T0334454

THE CALL OF CHARACTER

The Call of Character
Living a Life Worth Living

Mari Ruti

Columbia University Press
New York

Columbia University Press
Publishers Since 1893
New York   Chichester, West Sussex
cup.columbia.edu
Copyright © 2014 Mari Ruti

Library of Congress Cataloging-in-Publication Data
Ruti, Mari.
    The call of character : living a life worth living / Mari
Ruti.
        pages cm
    Includes bibliographical references and
    index. ISBN 978-0-231-16408-5 (cloth) —
    ISBN 978-0-231-53619-6 (e-book)
    1. Character.   2. Conduct of life.   I. Title.

BJ1521.R88   2013
170'.44—dc23   2013008069

Cover design by Mary Ann Smith
Cover photograph by Tetra Images

To AZ

I wrote this book for you before I even met you.

CONTENTS

PREFACE

One of the peculiarities of this book is that it presents relatively complex ideas in relatively simple language. I chose this approach because I believe that my topic—the question of what makes each of us a unique and idiosyncratic character—should be accessible to readers beyond the academy. At the same time, I have sought to avoid the overly simplistic tone of much of the popular writing on the theme. When self-help or New Age gurus tackle the question of what it means to lead a fulfilling life, the kind of life that feels worth living, they tend to advocate a streamlined program of (concrete or spiritual) steps that is supposed to lead to a harmonious existence, thereby sidestepping all the ways in which human life is not designed to be harmonious. Likewise, they tend to fall back on an untheorized notion of what it means to be a human being in the first place, talking as if the matter were completely straight-forward. It's not. As a result, if this book has a goal, it is to remain faithful to the complexities of human life without resorting to the mystifications of specialized academic idiom.

Three interventions run throughout this book that are meant to counter the manner in which the so-called good life is usually discussed in our culture. The first asserts that self-cultivation is not a matter of nurturing an essential core of being that makes us who we are, but rather of dwelling in the world in ways that allow us to add ever new layers of meaning into an identity that is always in the process of forming itself. That is, I start from the premise that our self is not a private possession (or achievement), but rather something we construct gradually through our engagement with our surroundings, including other people. Second, I argue that our quest for existential equilibrium is not only largely unrealistic, but perhaps also somewhat undesirable—that there may be something quite hollow about our cultural ideal of a balanced, composed, and unruffled life. Pointing out that sometimes it is the most tormented lives that are also the most rewarding, I propose that there might be advantages to a life that is a little neurotic but also hugely ardent and committed. Third, I posit that there is an almost astonishing specificity to human desire and that it is precisely this specificity that underpins our attempts to actualize our character. I believe that the more alienated we are from this specificity—from what the French psychoanalyst Jacques Lacan called the "truth" of our desire—the more alienated we also are from our character. Conversely, the more loyal we stay to this specificity, the better we are able to resist the dominant social norms that strive to suppress our character.

I evoke Lacan's name in part to alert the reader to the fact that many of the insights of this book are indebted to his thinking. But I also evoke it in order to render concrete the main rhetorical dilemma of this book—namely, that it draws on the work of some of the most demanding theorists of the previous century while at the same time trying to maintain a mainstream-friendly tone. Not only is this combination hard to achieve, but it raises some thorny conceptual concerns. Thinkers in my field—contemporary theory—tend to be proud of the impenetrability of its rhetoric, and with good reason, for they see this impenetrability as a theoretical intervention in its own right; exasperated by the notion that meaning should be transparent and easy to process, they often intentionally create an opaque textual surface in order to force the reader to grapple with the ways in which meaning is never obvious but open to a variety of interpretations. One might even say that there is an ethics of a sort to this willful opacity in the sense that it seeks to challenge the lenses we customarily use to comprehend the world, thus opening a space for alternative lenses, alternative points of view. I have a deep-seated respect for this attitude. Yet I also admit to being increasingly impatient with texts whose convoluted rhetoric hides the fact that the concepts being formulated are not, in the final analysis, very difficult at all. When I feel that I can state in twenty-five pages of clear prose what a book I am reading spends three hundred torturous pages articulating, I experience an exasperation of my own. This exasperation is one of the motivating factors of this book: it explains, in part, why I have made the rhetorical choices I have.

One might say that my deliberately lucid prose is my little act of defiance, my way of heeding the call of my character, for I never feel as connected to my writing as when I adopt this style. The second component of the book that grates against the conventions of my field is its understated but irrepressible hopefulness. For personal reasons—having to do with a relatively painful history of both material and emotional deprivation—I have never been able to fully accept contemporary theory's insistence on our lack of agency and disempowerment in relation to the world. Simply put, I have not been able to afford the idea that I have no way of actively improving my lot. At the same time, experience has taught me what I repeatedly communicate in this book—namely, that there is a difference between, on the one hand, the facile notions of self-improvement and "positive thinking" that circulate so widely in our culture and, on the other, the act of mindfully stepping into the cadence of a complicated life; I have learned that the easy answers that crowd our collective space have no teeth, that they cannot even begin to bite into the formidable and often genuinely frightening endeavor of living, relating, and—let's not forget about this—carrying on when we no longer see the point of it all. Particularly when it comes to experiences that cause us suffering, our culture's easy answers are almost patronizing in their cheerfulness. This is why the optimism of this book is cautious and keenly aware of its limits. And it is also why its propositions are tentative at best, shying away from the insincere certainties of prescriptive thought.

A discerning reader will already have noticed that the distinction between the terms *self, identity,* and *character* remains somewhat ambiguous. I am going to let that ambiguity stand, for I trust that the appropriate nuances will arise contextually from the arguments I will be presenting. But it may help to know that of these terms, *self* is the broadest, often encompassing the other two. *Identity,* in turn, includes both our private everyday sense of who we are and our social persona—the culturally intelligible personality that others relate to. Finally, *character* is what in many ways resists the confines of sociality, expressing, instead, something about the most eccentric frequencies of our being. It is out of a tentative deference for the latter—as well as, perhaps, out of the realization that it may still be somewhat difficult for female thinkers to claim their distinctive voice—that I have chosen to write this book with few quotations and references. This choice of course does not mean that the ideas contained in it have arisen in a vacuum. They have developed over a decade of engagement with the work of others, and I have done my best to point the reader to some of the most important influences in my notes. These notes, however, are insufficient to capture the full extent of my indebtedness to the multitude of borrowed thoughts that seep into my prose. Readers interested in a more detailed account of how my work intersects with that of others are invited to consult my more academic books.[1]

This book is divided into three sections, each of which focuses on a slightly different aspect of what it means to be called to one's character. Part I looks at the art of self-fashioning by arguing that the specificity of our character reflects the specificity of our desire. I propose that it is impossible to honor our character without honoring the distinctive contours of our desire and that this is the case even when our desire seems utterly irrational or socially inconvenient. Our desire—our impulse to reach out into the world in quest of things that might satisfy us—may render us vulnerable to injury, but it also ensures that we do not settle into a fixed definition of who we are; it ensures that the meaning of our lives remains malleable and open-ended. And insofar as it arises from the always idiosyncratic way in which we experience loss and deprivation, it gives rise to a code of conduct that can be quite different from prevailing social values, thereby making it possible for us to resist our culture's attempts to dictate the parameters of our behavior. To express the matter plainly, when the specificity of our desire is activated, we no longer care about what others think we should desire but feel compelled to obey the enigmatic directive of our own desire.

Part II looks at the art of self-responsibility by positing that the specificity of our desire makes us deeply responsible for the well-being of those who are its objects. In our society, it is common to assume that we cannot be held fully accountable for the portion of our desire that remains unconscious. In contrast, I assert that the fact that our actions are often unconsciously motivated does not absolve us of responsibility for the suffering we might inflict on others. I maintain that if we are repeatedly driven to hurt others in the same way, a big part of claiming a character is the ability to recognize such repetitive patterns and to learn to intervene in them before they cause devastation in the lives of others. The flipside of this is the realization that who we are—the distinctiveness of our character—has a great deal to do with how we have been injured, so that owning the full weight of our character is, to some extent, a matter of owning the full weight of the personal traumas that populate our past. The key to the good life, in other words, is not the ability to avoid pain, but rather the capacity to metabolize it so that we become capable of a more rewarding relationship to ourselves. This capability, in turn, allows us to develop a more rewarding relationship to others, including those we relate to intimately.

Part III looks at the art of self-surrender by examining events that—however fleetingly—transport us beyond the banalities of everyday life. Such events can feel life altering, as when we, for example, fall in love or are summoned to a creative, political, or professional destiny that we never imagined for ourselves. But they can also be as seemingly minor as learning to observe the details of our life-world from an unfamiliar perspective. "Transcendence," according to this view, does not require that we leave the world behind, but merely that we agree to experience it in a new way. In the first of these instances, we are invited to translate life's unpredictable swerves into a calling of some kind. And we are asked to cope with a degree of upheaval, which is exactly why anxiety—and particularly the capacity to bear the uncertainties and ambivalences of existence—tends to be an intrinsic component of a life that feels worth living. In the second instance, we are invited to translate life's more mundane stretches into something personally resonant. We may, for instance, choose to embrace the kinds of experiences—frequently broadly erotic in nature—that cause us to lose track of our customary way of being in the world; we may find ourselves ushered beyond our social persona to the elusive edges of immediate self-experience. Both of these modalities of self-surrender, I suggest, can potentially contribute to the articulation of our character.

ACKNOWLEDGMENTS

I thank my amazing editors at Columbia University Press—Lauren Dockett, Anne McCoy, Jennifer Perillo, and Stephen Wesley—and copyeditor Annie Barva for their bold support for the kind of writing that I have opted for in this book as well as in *The Summons of Love* (published by the press in 2011).

Thanks also to my agent, Elizabeth Evans, for her continued faith in my ability to keep inventing new modes of writing.

Finally, an immense thanks to the highly motivated (and motivating) students—both at Harvard and the University of Toronto—who have taught me to cut through the shroud of impenetrable rhetoric to the passion of the ideas beneath it. I would not have been able to write this book had I not spent two decades in the classroom distilling seemingly inaccessible concepts into something more accessible. That said, my biggest appreciation is reserved for those students who have understood that sometimes such distillation is impossible—that there are times when the only thing to be done is to respect the text's resistance to being mastered in the usual sense of the term.

THE CALL OF CHARACTER

PART I

THE ART OF
SELF-FASHIONING

1

The Call of Character

Some things are in some real sense really you, or express what
you are, and others aren't.

—Bernard Williams

1

The question of how to live a life worth living has an illustrious
history in our society, for leading philosophers, psychologists, the-
ologians, and artists have grappled with it at least since Socrates.
But what sets our era apart from earlier ones is that our relationship to this question is deeply ambivalent. On the one hand, we
are no longer sure if it's worth asking. We know (or strongly suspect) that God is dead,[1] that Truth with the capital T is difficult
to attain, that the universe is a chaotic place, that the world is a
violent mess, and that there may not be any final purpose to our
lives. What, then, would be the benefit of dwelling on the overall
validity of the life path we have chosen (or been thrown into)?
And given the enormous trials faced by the world—war, hunger,
poverty, social inequality, environmental damage, and so on—isn't

there something fairly selfish about such navel gazing to begin with? Wouldn't it be better to spend our energies on trying to solve problems that actually have a solution?

What is more, the utilitarian ethos of our culture can make us a little ashamed of squandering our resources on something as purely speculative as the question of what constitutes a life worth living: we are supposed to be productive rather than contemplative. We are asked to embrace the practical concerns of our lives, such as professional goals, family matters, and trips to the mall, without worrying too much about their ultimate significance. Indeed, many of us have internalized the idea that feeling too ardently about anything—including the merit of our existence—is a waste of time in the sense that nothing we do makes much of a difference. We are beyond grand ideals, grand passions, as well as personal or political acts of courage. Whenever we catch ourselves getting too stirred up about anything—even if it's just the thrilling date we had on Saturday night—we back away, for we know that irrational ardor is . . . well, irrational. In a way, level-headed pragmatism has replaced the enthusiasm of higher aspirations so that many of us spend our lives trying to enjoy the ride as long as it lasts without investing ourselves too strongly in anything. Investments, after all, are never entirely reliable.

On the other hand, many of us yearn to feel fully alive. We want to feel "real" and "authentic," connected to the deepest recesses of our being; we want to feel that there is a point to our existence. Even the utilitarian tenor of our society cannot entirely banish the little voice inside of us that keeps asking about the meaning of it all. This voice may not trouble us too often. But it tends to surface at key moments in our lives—for example, when something goes drastically wrong, when things seem unusually difficult, when someone we love dies or faces hardship, when the dismal state of the world jolts us out of our complacency, or when we get a vivid reminder of our own mortality. During such times, it is easy to feel helpless, for our society does not offer much guidance.

Those who are religious may draw strength from their faith, but the rest of us find ourselves on a desperate quest for meaning in a world that seems hopelessly devoid of it. There are those who turn to the self-help or New Age shelf for answers. Others pledge allegiance to Western "tradition," in some cases through a return to the classics of art, music, literature, and philosophy, in others through a conservative turn to "timeless" values. Yet others immerse themselves in political action, trying to change the world one step at a time. And a large portion of us bury ourselves in our work, families, relationships, private worries, and television screens so as to avoid the question altogether. Yet it persists: it silently but stubbornly nibbles at the edges of our consciousness.

In this book, I would like to give this voice a fair hearing. And I would like to show that heeding its summons—what I have chosen to conceptualize as the call of our character—is not antithetical to social responsibility, but rather an essential component of our ability to care for others as well as for the world at large. That is, the seemingly personal question of how we are going to live our lives is inherently ethical so that whenever we ask it, we are automatically concerned about our relationship to the complex backdrop of our existence; we are by default interested not only in the self, but also in the self's attitude toward what surrounds and sustains it. Perhaps most fundamentally, I would like to illustrate that, contrary to what one might expect, our inability to find the ultimate meaning of our lives is not an existential tragedy, but rather an asset of enormous proportions.

By *existential*, I am not referring to anything too esoteric. I am simply talking about the basic building blocks of human life—about how we go about making pivotal decisions about the contours of our existence. *Existential*, in other words, is an umbrella term for indicating that we are dealing with the fundamentals of human experience: where we seek meaning and value; what we find important and worthy of our effort; how we meet life's inevitable challenges, adversities, and bursts of agony; how we respond to the obstacles and opportunities we encounter; how we determine which goals, activities, ambitions, or people warrant our attention and which do not; how we love, hate, or simply ignore those close to us; how and where we find pleasure, enjoyment, fulfillment, or a sense of self-actualization; what satisfies us and what does not; and where (or to whom) we turn when all else fails. According to this account, more or less anything having to do with how we opt (or feel compelled) to live our lives is "existential." But there is perhaps nothing more so than our questions about why we are here, what we are supposed to accomplish, and where we, in the final analysis, are headed. The question "How should I live?" may seem simple. But in many ways it represents the pinnacle of human endeavors to make sense of their lives as well as of the world in which they struggle to carve out their individual destinies.

2

When I say that our inability to find the ultimate meaning of our lives is an existential asset, I am not trying to trick or frustrate you. Rather, I am trying to shift your perspective so that you come to see that it is precisely the *lack* of clear-cut answers to life-defining questions that makes human existence so fascinating. For one thing, it is because we do not know what the best way to live is that we keep trying to figure it out; it is because we cannot solve the conundrum of human experience that we feel motivated to give it our best shot. If the meaning of our lives were handed to us on a silver platter, we would quickly lose interest in it. Chances are we might even rebel against it, insisting that there must be something "else" out there. As humans, we are designed to be curious: we are driven to peek over the fence, gaze into outer space, peer into the deepest abyss, wind our way around a barricade, stake our flag on a mountaintop, and investigate what eludes our grasp. We are, in sum, fated to want what we can't quite have (which is why our neighbor's grass is always greener). One might in fact argue that desire (wanting what we can't have) is the motor of human life, so that when desire comes to an end, so does life. Or, to be more precise, life in its innovative, forward-moving form requires the energizing nudge of desire.

This brings us to an interesting observation—namely, that many of the world's most powerful religions, from Christianity to

Buddhism, deem desire highly problematic. In Christianity, the original sin of humankind is the birth of desire (Eve and the apple). In Buddhism, desire is the root cause of pain and suffering. Moreover, the main goal of many strands of Western popular spirituality is to get rid of the ego and its selfish desires. But why should this be? Why does spirituality so often take the shape of trying to extinguish desire? Why is religiosity routinely accompanied by a revulsion toward desire?

One obvious reason is that desire tends to lead to gluttony. We don't always know where the line between satisfaction and greediness resides. And even when we do, we may find it hard to keep ourselves from crossing that line. Once our desire is in full swing, arresting its momentum can be virtually impossible, so that we never have enough of what we want: we want more food even though we have just had dinner; we want more money even though we have plenty of it; we want a bigger house even though our current one is spacious enough; we want more books even though our study is overflowing with ones we haven't had time to read. And we definitely want more love. No matter how much affection we get, we cannot quite seem to get enough of it. There is an endlessness to desire that is difficult to manage or curtail, which is why it is sometimes easier to kill it altogether than to temper its voraciousness; it is easier to slay the beast than to tame it. What many spiritual approaches have figured out is that the best way to restrain desire is to starve it to the point that it no longer has enough strength to raise its insatiable head.

In this restraint, spirituality finds a strange bedfellow in Western rationalism, which also aims to divest human life of the excesses of passion. From the tenets of scientific objectivity to disinterested principles of justice, rationalism relies on the notion that we must be able to expunge desire from our lives at those moments when we make decisions about true or false, right or wrong.[2] Desire, in short, is the enemy of both clear-headedness and evenhandedness. It muddles our judgment, making us see only what we want to see so that our knowledge claims cannot be trusted. And, even worse, it elevates those we love to a special status so that our ethical choices (about who should live and who can be left to die, who should be respected and who can be mistreated, who should receive assistance and who can be neglected, and so on) lose their impartiality, thereby becoming more or less useless. After all, an ethics that does not apply equally to everyone hardly merits being called an ethics.

I don't disagree with this view. But I would like to complicate the matter by raising three interrelated points. First, desire always has a way of snaking its way back into our lives so that the more we try to ignore, repress, or get around it, the more it tends to gain in intensity; the starvation diet all too easily generates uncontrollable binges so that, for instance, religious asceticism slides into the fanaticism of holy war. Second, desire's capacity to cloud our judgment is perhaps never as strong as when we pretend that it is not there; there is nothing that corrupts scientific or ethical results more than the claim that we are being objective when we in fact are not. Third, as much as science and justice defend against desire, they also need its vitalizing current to progress: objectivity devoid of passion may be the goal of both science and justice, but without passion there would be no movement toward this goal. The most groundbreaking scientists and lawmakers understand this, as do those politicians, leaders, educators, writers, painters, actors, activists, and other shapers of culture who have "vision" along with common sense. Or, to state the matter in a way directly applicable to this book's argument, desire is absolutely indispensable for the augmentation of our character.

3

But what does it mean to talk about "character" in the first place? The term easily brings to mind an image of a deep truth that makes a given person who he or she is. We tend to think of a person's character as his or her authentic self. And we often believe that this authenticity has been buried out of sight, perhaps because the person in question is somehow ashamed of it or because it has been forced into hiding by the hostilities and pressures of the external world. There is, in other words, a crucial distinction between our public "persona" and our "character," between our socially conformist (obedient) self and the singular (potentially rebellious) core of our identity. On this view, the existential task of each of us is to unveil our personal truth so that we can finally release our character from its prison cell; our mission is to free our suffocating essence from beneath the false (superficial) self-presentations we display to others. Through self-interrogation, we are supposed to become better attuned to the messages of our interiority so that we can learn to differentiate between our true desires and those that merely support our public roles (in the sense of being socially expected and encouraged). The hope here is that we gradually develop the ability to stay faithful to our true desires even when this costs us some of our social standing; the hope is that we come to respect the call of our character even when doing so complicates our lives.

I agree with much of this description, with one notable proviso. I do not believe that our character is a fixed core of being that once and for all dictates who we are. "Authenticity," in my opinion, is not a function of specific personality traits or attributes, but rather a mode of living and relating to the world; it is not some sort of a permanent truth of our being, but rather a matter of how we enter into the continuous process of transformation that characterizes human life. From this perspective, the quest for authenticity is less an attempt to liberate a hidden kernel of our being from some underground dungeon than a commitment to promote dimensions of ourselves that are still mere potentialities. It is less a question of closing the gap between our false self and the mysterious essence of our repressed character than of bridging the chasm between our current reality and what we have the potential to become.

To be sure, one might posit that pursuing the mysterious essence of our character is the same thing as pursuing our highest potential. But there is a difference in that the first of these approaches presupposes a ready-made and immutable truth of being that is merely a little hard to see (or interpret correctly), whereas the second assumes that our personal truth, and therefore our character, is always in the making; it assumes that our character can never be definitively named for the simple reason that it is continuously in the process of materializing or—as philosophers like to put it— of "becoming." That is, although our character can certainly be "cultivated" in the sense that it can be raised to a more complex expression (actualized on a more mature level), it is never "done." It is endlessly deferred, which is just another way of saying that it is never fully realized.

This is not to deny that we have latent qualities that can be profitably rescued from repression and brought into the light of day. It's just that these qualities do not ever congeal into a stable essence that would determine our character for all times to come. They are merely one component of a mobile and always slightly incomplete private reality. This is why I prefer to talk about authentic existential paths rather than about authentic personalities. Whereas the notion of an authentic personality remains bogged down in the idea of an innate self that never changes, the notion of an authentic existential path caters to the idea of a distinctive spirit (or even a "style") that makes us who we are—that lends our character its idiosyncratic uniqueness—without arresting us in a rigid definition of who we are supposed to be.

This unique spirit is what renders each of us unexchangeable and irreplaceable so that it is impossible to mistake, let alone substitute, one person for another; it explains why, to return to the words of Bernard Williams, "[s]ome things are in some real sense really you, or express what you are, and others aren't."[3] Furthermore, it has a historical awareness that recognizes that our past has shaped our present and that our present will impact our future. It makes each of us "us" while simultaneously acknowledging that who we are shifts over time, so that although there may be some continuity between our spirit at the age of sixteen and our spirit at the age of seventy-eight, it is also obvious that this spirit goes through many modifications during the decades that separate immaturity from maturity. If it did not, we would not be capable of cultivating our character; we would not be able to learn from our mistakes, add emotional density to our relationships, or acquire a more nuanced understanding of what really matters to us in life.

4

I have already hinted at the idea that our desire offers an excellent clue to which things are "really" us and which aren't, for some of our desires come much closer to staying faithful to our spirit than others. If desire is the motor of human life, as I suggested earlier, then no two motors are exactly alike. Some are slower than others; some take time to warm up, whereas others are ready to go at full speed in a matter of seconds. Likewise, where our desire finds satisfaction is highly personal, so that what intrigues us might bore others and vice versa. Once again, this does not mean that our desire is fixed for life—that it is not capable of finding new objects. But insofar as there is a degree of consistency to our spirit, there is also a degree of consistency to our desire so that some things are better at fulfilling our cravings than others. I am not talking here about preferring chocolate ice cream over vanilla, or about liking younger men more than older ones, though these things can also be important. Rather, I am talking about the enigmatic specificity of desire that urges us to follow certain life directions rather than others—that repeatedly induces us to take certain kinds of actions rather than others. I return to this specificity in chapter 3. For now, it is important to realize that when we cannot find a way to honor this specificity—when our satisfactions do not match the uniqueness of our desire—we risk losing our vitality; we risk feeling that our lives have ceased to be meaningful.

Many people these days complain that they do not feel fully alive—that they do not feel sufficiently attached to the world or to their own lives. They complain about a kind of deadness of soul or a dreadful sluggishness of spirit.[4] They go through the motions of life and may even accomplish a great deal in terms of professional ambitions or solid relationships, yet something is missing. There is an underlying futility to their existence that makes them feel "fake" or not fully "present" in their skins. Much of the time, they sense that the edition of themselves they display to the world and even to themselves is a hollow shell, front, mask, or cloak that may sometimes even dazzle but does not ultimately bring fulfillment. Sometimes this feeling of unreality is physical, having to do with a profound disconnection from one's bodily actuality. Other times it is psychological and emotional so that even though one may have many thoughts and sentiments, these thoughts and sentiments seem to be separated from the self by some sort of a translucent barrier. They are there, but they are not linked to any real passion. They do not feed the spirit, but rather alienate the self from an authenticity of experience.

This disconnect makes it all the more noteworthy that so many of us are accustomed to approach our lives with a sensible practicality stripped of the disorienting (irrational) impact of desire. We are trained to mistrust desire not only in those areas of life, such as science and justice, where such mistrust is prudent, but also in those, such as our private existential struggles, where doing so can only sap our life force. Even when we recognize—as many of us do—that desire is the seed of creativity, that without desire life loses much of its vigor, our passion tends to make us nervous. We know that the more space we give to desire, the less stable our lives tend to be. And because we associate instability with trepidation, and trepidation with unhappiness, we are often willing to go to great lengths to ensure that our realism trumps our ardor. There is no doubt that there are times when this is the right course of action, when rational deliberation prevents us from making mistakes that would be too costly. And it can even keep us from hurting those we love. Yet there is also a considerable downside—namely, that the attempt to smother desire can rob us of our biggest resource for fostering lives that feel multidimensional and thus worth living: it can make it impossible for us to hear the call of our character.

The vague existential malaise that plagues many of us can be a sign that there is a fundamental misalignment between desire and satisfaction; there is too large a gulf between the longings of the spirit and the mundane realities of daily life. Repression—being scared of our passion—is one obvious explanation for this misalignment. But it may also be that we are for one reason or another incapable of accurately reading our desire, perhaps because we have never learned to do so or because we have been overrun by social norms to such an extent that our desire gets swallowed up by the kinds of desires that our culture would like us to have. It would in fact be difficult to overestimate the degree to which we tend to adopt desires that saturate the social space around us. As soon as we enter the world, we are bombarded by networks of culturally condoned desire that train us to want what everyone else wants, so that it becomes virtually impossible for us to tell the difference between desires that originate from our private universe and ones that originate from the pool of publicly sanctioned yearnings. Indeed, when it comes to desire, the boundary between the private and the public is so blurry that it may not even make sense to talk about individual versus collective desires; it may well be that much of what we think of as our private world has been modeled after the public domain. This is exactly what the advertising industry relies on: when we covet a specific product or admire a specific individual (say, a movie star or a singer), it is in large part because we have been programmed to do so.

At the same time, humans are not automatons. We possess the capacity for various forms of resistance so that even if it is impossible for us to completely dissociate our desires from the desires of the collectivity, there are still degrees of freedom and unfreedom: there are degrees of originality and unoriginality. This is why I have begun to suggest that our sense of authenticity has to do with the fit between our desires and the distinctive aspirations of our spirit. More concretely, one might say that it has to do with the correlation between our desires and our ideals. A desire, after all, is frequently an (as yet) unattained ideal—a potential that might become a reality. As a result, whenever we pursue desires that support our ideals, we feel real. But when we fail to do so, we feel that we are being disloyal to our potential. Our unease signals that we need to work at creating a better correspondence between our desires and ideals and that we need to do so even when our ideals happen to deviate from those of the cultural establishment. This is why the authenticity of our character is linked to our ability to "own" our desires—to follow the pulse of our passion even when doing so means going against what our society reckons appropriate. It is why there is often something (explicitly or implicitly) countercultural about our character, why it is impossible to talk about character without talking about the inherent rebelliousness of passion.

5

But even this way of putting things does not do full justice to the issue at hand, for what I have been loosely calling our "passion" is not just a matter of desire, but also of bodily drives— of elemental energies that tend to be even more amorphous and hard to pin down than desire. Desire may sometimes feel "crazy making" in the sense that it is always to some extent beyond our control. But it is still more orderly—more coherent and consistent—than the drives. Precisely because there is a historicity to our desire, it is to some degree knowable: although our desire can certainly surprise us, much of the time we have some sense of how it is going to manifest itself. This is less so with the drives. I do not mean that they have completely escaped cultural conditioning—that they are something akin to the biological instincts of other animals. Humans are so thoroughly social that even what seems most straightforwardly biological may not in fact be so in any pure sense: because our biological processes always interact with the cultural environment within which we live, it is difficult to completely detangle them from external stimuli (for instance, a neck ache may be a biological phenomenon, but there is often a social cause for it). However, the socialization of the drives has not reached nearly the same level of organization as desire has, so that when the drives get the better of us—when our biological processes overwhelm our defenses—we can get agitated to the point of not being able to function properly.[5]

I noted earlier that one reason we tend to flee from our passion is that it makes it harder for us to feel calm and collected. We are now in a better position to understand the full implications of this. If our character expresses not only the unruliness of our desire, but also the even greater unruliness of our drives, it is clear that whenever we truly hear its call, we risk losing our composure; we risk having to put up with many volatile and potentially embarrassing excesses that mortify the more polished parts of our being. The price we pay for feeling "real" is a degree of existential bewilderment so that the more faithful we remain to our character, the more we need to learn to tolerate whatever sticks out of, undermines, or refuses to be disciplined into the seamless persona that sustains our social viability. This is not easy, for we are conditioned to read agitation—what we often describe by the diffuse label of "anxiety"—as a personal failure, as a fatal flaw in the otherwise reasonable surface of our existence. Even though agitation may be a precondition of our capacity to actualize our character, it is difficult for us to eliminate the idea that there is something drastically wrong with us when we cannot prevent our passion from overflowing the dams that are meant to contain it.

It doesn't help that we live in a culture that overvalues serenity. Although the rushed pace of contemporary life makes tranquility more and more impossible to come by, we are constantly warned against the pitfalls of anxiety, including the psychosomatic symptoms it is supposed to spawn. These warnings are in fact so pervasive that it is hard not to feel anxious about feeling anxious. Wellness "experts" and spiritual gurus alike tell us that agitation is bad for us. Obviously this is true in that there is a difference between feeling genuinely alive and electrified, on the one hand, and feeling restless and hyperactive, on the other. But I would still say that there is something suspicious about the idea that a balanced life is automatically better than one that is a little lopsided and anxiety ridden but also genuinely passionate.[6] Sometimes the worst we can do is to maintain our balance at the expense of our ardor, for ardor—along with the anxiety that it often generates—is what keeps us connected to our character; it keeps us from sliding into complacency and becoming a mere cog in the cultural machine that does its best to level distinctions between individuals.

6

Although our society pays a lot of lip service to individuality, the fact is that the more similar we are to each other, the better from the standpoint of utilitarian efficiency. When those in positions of political and economic power know what to expect from us, it is easier for them to sell us everything from opinions to beauty products. It is when we become unpredictable that things become dicey. As a consequence, the more we hold on to our idiosyncratic passions, the more difficult we make it for the political and economic establishment to run its business as usual; the more we insist on the integrity of our ideals and desires, the less receptive we are to the ideals and desires that the collective order makes available to us, with the result that we become harder to control, harder to brainwash.

From this viewpoint, the notion that we need to lead healthy and well-adjusted lives may be somewhat overrated. Why is a healthy and well-adjusted life superior to one that is filled with personal vision but is also at times a little unhealthy and maladjusted? Might some of us not prefer lives that are heaving with an intensity of feeling and action but that do not last quite as long as those that follow a more sensible organization? Why should the good life equal a harmonious life? Might not the good life rather be one that includes just the right amount of anxiety? Isn't anxiety (along with desire) what propels us forward, thereby keeping us from stagnating? And isn't a degree of tension a precondition of our ability to recognize tranquility when we are lucky enough to encounter it? In a slightly different vein, why should our lives be cautious rather than a little dangerous? Might the best lives not be ones where we sometimes allow ourselves to become a little imprudent or even a tad unhinged?

I recently attended a presentation given by the daughter of a very prominent man—a man who wrote a number of paradigm-shifting books that have had a tremendous impact on how we understand human psychology. During her talk, the daughter faulted her (now dead) father for not having been a stable "family man," for having let his enthusiasm for his work overshadow the rest of his life, and for having never been completely at ease with everyday social interactions. She made it sound as if her father had been a failure of a person because he had not been able to appreciate the rewards of a well-adjusted life. As I listened to her, I kept thinking that she was judging her father by a very conventional standard. As far as I am concerned, there are situations where the ability to show up at the dinner table is less important than the capacity to produce works of great genius that enrich the rest of society. Indeed, many of the people who have made the biggest contributions to our collective history—intellectuals, researchers, composers, writers, artists, and so on—have lived lives that from the outside seem fairly pathological. They have often been deeply solitary, have had trouble forming enduring relationships, have been consumed by their projects to the point of obsession, have plunged into the depths of depression and despair, have doubted and disparaged themselves, and have had to endure the coldness and sharpness of the world's judgment.[7] Yet who is to say that these lives are somehow less poignant than those that seem more wholesome?

When it comes to heeding the call of one's character, it is possible that these "pathological" lives have come closer to authenticity than many more stable ones. If I state the issue so strongly, it is because I want to call attention to the thoroughly ideological nature of our often absolutely uncontested faith in the value of poise and equanimity. If we had grown up in a different society, we might celebrate other traits instead—say, heroism, courage, or absolute dedication to a cause. By this argument, I do not wish to valorize psychological or emotional instability. I am well aware of the enormous toll it can exact. And I know that there are many people in our society who belabor under unbearable burdens of uncertainty—a point I address in greater detail later. But I think that we are mistaken when we interpret existential bewilderment as something entirely external to the desirable life. From the perspective of character development, crises and bouts of disequilibrium may well be an essential part of the process rather than its undoing. Likewise, there is perhaps nothing that contributes to the uniqueness of our character more than our suffering. In so many ways, who we are arises from how we have been hurt. This does not mean that we cannot find our way past our injuries or that they determine our future. But it does suggest that our sense of authenticity cannot be divorced from the hardships and disappointments we have endured. I would in fact go as far as to say that those who have borne a great deal of pain may have garnered a more panoramic understanding of the human predicament than those who haven't.

7

I don't want to equate authenticity with sugarcoated notions of well-being, for there are times when being able to feel pain is a way to remain self-connected. Understood in this manner, authenticity is not a matter of existential comfort but rather connotes the kind of inner capaciousness that can accommodate a variety of conflicting affective states, including those that feel utterly uncomfortable. Closely related to this is the idea with which I began—namely, that our inability to locate the ultimate purpose of our lives does not imply that there is no meaning, that our lives lack luster, or that we cannot find value in the world. It merely means that sometimes we have to work quite hard to locate this meaning, luster, or value; it means that we cannot expect anyone to deliver our life's mission to our doorstep but must actively look for it in the place where the self meets the world. In the pages that follow, I talk about just how messy this place can get, for there is nothing as convoluted as the interface between the individual and the collective. This is in part because the collective is always already embedded within the individual and in part because the individual can, in greater or lesser degrees, alter the parameters of the collective. Sometimes it takes just one person—say, a Rosa Parks, a Mahatma Gandhi, an

Albert Einstein, or even an Oprah Winfrey—to change world history. More commonly, our influence does not extend beyond the network of relationships that constitute the intimate circle of our lives. But this does not change the fact that if the world shapes us, we also shape the world.

There are those who bemoan the loss of "tradition"—who see the demise of definitive meaning and social hierarchy as an indication that civilization is in decline. From their point of view, order has been replaced by anarchy, stability by randomness. And because they do not recognize (or because they refuse to admit) the oppressive side of "tradition"—the fact that it brutally excluded those who did not fall neatly within its borders—they do their best to artificially reinstate this order and stability, sometimes through fundamentalist forms of religion, other times through a reaffirmation of bigotry (so that, once again, women are inferior, gays are perverts, blacks are criminals, Arabs are terrorists, and immigrants are out to steal the jobs of "real people"). My goal in this book, in contrast, is to demonstrate that the crumbling of definitive meaning does not impoverish us—that our awareness that the "point" of human existence always remains a little mysterious should not keep us from leading rewarding lives. Rather, it invites us to spin intricate tapestries of personalized meaning that lend weightiness to our existence. In this sense, the lack of authoritative meaning is the underpinning of our ability to fashion more partial (yet potentially powerful) meanings, so that the collapse of tradition is not a sign of civilization's breakdown but, quite the opposite, of the growing resourcefulness of the human race. After all, it is much more demanding, and thus much more valiant, to cope with an ambiguity of meaning than to robotically endorse (seemingly) straightforward values.

Coping with an ambiguity of meaning asks that we bring a degree of conscious deliberation to the process of figuring out how we want to proceed. And it requires that we find our own answers to life's central questions instead of relying on those provided by external authorities. Indeed, the lack of obvious, reassuring, or universal answers to our questions by no means annuls the importance of these questions but rather makes them all the more urgent: the lack of easy answers does not mean that no answers are available to us. I would in fact say that our yearning for easy answers may well be our biggest stumbling block, for it can keep us from finding the sorts of answers that are not entirely self-evident but that are nevertheless personally meaningful to us. Such answers may not hold much value for others. But as long as they resonate with the unique passions of our spirit, they make our lives feel worth living. And over time our continued capacity to keep asking the right kinds of questions, as well as to keep discovering responses that in one way or another galvanize us, gives us the tools to remake our lives so that who we become tomorrow may be very different from who we are today. The call of our character is what makes such transformation possible, what gives us the push to keep rewriting our story line until we hit upon something that feels "right" (for the time being at least). This book is about that call—about the often quite inscrutable directive that summons us to become who we are meant to be.

2

The Process of Becoming

We, however, *want to become those we are*—human beings who are new, unique, incomparable, who give themselves laws, who create themselves.

—Friedrich Nietzsche

1

How do we, as Nietzsche puts it, become who we are? When it comes to answering this question, two approaches vie for domination. The first is that "we are who we are"—that we were born a certain way and this is what we are stuck with; we may gradually be able to refine the inner core that makes us who we are, but the outline of our lives is determined from the get-go, well before we formulate our first sentence.[1] The second approach—the one I have already started to explore because I believe it is the more accurate as well as the more interesting of the two—is that we are always in the process of becoming and that it is our existential task to cultivate the unique character that gains momentum from our continuous engagement with this process; it is our responsibility to actualize our potential by tending the spirit that, in an always provisional manner, makes us who we are. As I have pointed out, this spirit expresses something about the idiosyncratic intonation of our desire, which is why cultivating our character does not always make us the most submissive (or well-adjusted) members of society. And it can even lead to high levels of anxiety that render us restless. But it connects us to the particularities of our passion so that we can experiment with what it means, on the concrete level, to be "incomparable."

I don't deny that we are born with certain tendencies: talents, abilities, limitations, and weaknesses. But even if this is true, it is simply not the case that our personalities are set in stone at birth. Our character or distinctive spirit is not something we inherit from the gods, but rather something we fashion through our ongoing interactions both with the constraints of our own constitution and with the constraints of the external world. We cannot choose our biological or neurological composition any more than we can choose to be born beautiful. We cannot choose our race, gender, or social class, and we cannot single-handedly change how our culture responds to such markers of identity. And we also cannot choose the time, place, family, and upbringing we are born into. In this sense, we are inserted into a nexus of restraints that to some extent determine the life-directions that are open to us. This is why the idea that we all can become whatever we want to become—an idea promoted by the American dream as well as by some of the more facile strands of popular psychology—is overly optimistic at best and insidious at worst, for it is not always possible for us to overcome the restrictions that are imposed on us. To state the issue bluntly, wanting to be X usually doesn't make us so, regardless of how many self-help guides we consume.

But neither are we the helpless victims of our destinies. The characteristics we are born with and the conditions we are thrown into shape our life-world, giving us a specific set of obstacles and opportunities, but much depends on how we meet that world; much depends on how dexterously we bring together the particulars of our constitution and the particulars of our environment. In the same way that a river takes a certain shape in relation to the landscape that surrounds it, at times yielding to rocks and other obstructions on its course, at other times rushing down steep precipices to form stunning waterfalls, human beings evolve in response to outside influences. And in the same way that a river can get disoriented by a bunch of beavers building a dam, humans can get disoriented by unanticipated hindrances (what we like to call "problems") on their path. A great deal, then, depends on the kinds of openings and barriers we encounter as well as on how we approach these openings and barriers. The fact that we don't have absolute freedom to become whoever we want to doesn't mean that we have no freedom at all; it just means that we need to learn to exercise this freedom within certain constraints.

This is what Nietzsche has in mind when he urges us to become who we are, when he tells us to become the kinds of human beings who "create themselves."[2] He is not talking about resurrecting a buried core of personality, but rather about an ongoing art of living that allows us to craft a distinctive character out of the obstacles and opportunities that constitute the key components of our existence. According to Nietzsche, we all are invited to become the poets of our lives, individuals who "give themselves laws" (dictate their own life direction) within the parameters of their particular fate. Even the so-called mistakes we make—the wrong turns we take—can become material for our acts of self-fashioning. In this sense, there is nothing about our lives that is "just" a blunder or a misstep, for such failings are an essential part of our destiny. And sometimes they may even work in our favor, provided we have the patience to wait for their message to unfurl. It may, for example, turn out that something that causes us suffering will eventually grow into a nugget of wisdom that guides us to a valuable course adjustment. And a breakdown that leaves us gasping for air can eventually lead to an important breakthrough that reconfigures our lives for the better. This is why Nietzsche believes that we should choose to love our fate—that instead of struggling against the constraints of our situation, we should actively welcome these constraints because they are the foundation of our ability to elaborate our character.

There are of course situations where this vision does not hold—where the suffering in question far exceeds what is "normal" in human life, so that it becomes problematic to ask those undergoing it to "love" their fates. I return to this point later. For now, it is useful to recognize that Nietzsche's way of conceptualizing self-development implies that our character is not a wholly private, introspective undertaking, but something we form through our complex relationship to the world. From this perspective, what makes us unique are not the attributes we were born with, but how we bring these attributes in contact with outside influences, including other people. This is exactly why human life is so unreliable, for we can never determine ahead of time what kinds of influences we will come across; we can never decide once and for all what kinds of people we will become because we cannot control the aspects of the world we will brush against along the way. Although we have a fair amount of say over how we interact with the world—which is why we are able to embark on the task of becoming the poets of our lives in the first place—we cannot ever completely stage-manage it to our satisfaction. Sometimes the world is piercingly hostile. Other times it is warm and welcoming. Inasmuch as we learn from experience, our attempts to predict how the chips will fall may over time become more accurate. But they are never foolproof, which is why our quest for existential certainty is always to some degree pointless—why we are rarely as misguided as when we declare that we have finally figured out the ultimate meaning of our lives.

2

The idea that we develop specific characters, specific personal profiles, because of our exposure to the world is at once incredibly simple and incredibly far reaching. Think about how drastically different human life would be if our bodies, psyches, and spirits were self-contained rather than permeable. Think about how straightforward things would be if we in fact *were* born with a fixed character and a predetermined destiny—if we were to know from the onset how our lives are supposed to turn out. It is precisely our radical openness to the world that complicates things for us. For one thing, it makes us unspeakably vulnerable to suffering. Whether our pain results from accidentally bumping our elbow on the sharp corner of our desk, from the wounding words of someone we love, or from a racist image we see in a magazine, the world has a way of getting under our skin. And the closer we are to the world's violence, the greater the potential for damage, so that there is a huge difference between witnessing racism from a distance, on the one hand, and being its direct object, on the other. Similarly, there is a difference between watching the evening news to follow the destructive unfolding of a tsunami or a military mission and finding oneself in the midst of such events.

One might say that there are two different levels of vulnerability. The first impacts all human beings universally in the sense that all of us have bodies, psyches, and spirits that can be reached—and sometimes violated—by the outside world. On the bodily level, even those of us who are not subject to extreme violence such as war, torture, or domestic abuse can find our surroundings difficult to handle. We often develop psychosomatic symptoms, such as muscle pain or insomnia, in response to feeling that we are constantly under assault by our environment. Even something as simple as sitting in rush-hour traffic or battling the long lines in a bank or grocery store can grate our nerves. And the repeated act of making it through the demands of the work day can drain us to such an extent that we become exhausted by the very idea of putting one foot in front of the other. Likewise, the cutting words or actions of parents, friends, lovers, partners, and colleagues can terrorize us psychologically and emotionally, sometimes crushing our spirit so thoroughly that we start to question our basic worth. When a parent says something mean or a lover treats us cruelly, it is easy to start doubting our very right to exist. It is astonishing, really, that people have so much power over each other—that we care so much about what other people say or do.

What is more, there are things—illnesses and sudden accidents—against which there is no protection. All of this leads me to think that it would be judicious to admit that the world will always find its way into our inner sanctum, that no matter how effectively we shield ourselves against it, it tends to devise new ways to wound and sometimes even defeat us. Again, I am not saying that we are entirely powerless against the world. But we might as well acknowledge our relative helplessness in relation to it. This helplessness is most pronounced in infancy, when we are completely dependent on our parents or other caretakers for our very survival. Those who care for us may treat us lovingly. But they may also abuse their power, mishandle us in various ways, or neglect our essential needs. Similarly, as adults, we are enmeshed in networks of power and interpersonal complexity that infiltrate our bodily, psychological, and spiritual composition with varying degrees of impact. And in old age, we are frequently ravaged by both physical erosion and emotional terror about our own mortality. As a consequence, whenever we try to conjure away our constitutive vulnerability, be it through belligerent cries of self-sufficiency or the rhetoric of spiritual "enlightenment" (to cite two obvious examples), we are not being entirely truthful with ourselves; we are trying to deny that our resistance to the world's intrusiveness is always limited.

The second level of vulnerability is not universal but context specific and contingent. It is made up of aspects of human life that are unevenly distributed so that some of us lead lives that are much more precarious than others. I am referring to things such as hunger, poverty, racism, sexism, homophobia, parental or spousal abuse, the devastations of war, political dictatorship, ethnic cleansings, as well as rape, assault, and torture. It is important for us to reflect on the difference between the kind of universal vulnerability I have outlined and this kind of more selective vulnerability; it is essential to recognize the distinction between the general privations of life, on the one hand, and intolerable cruelty, oppression, humiliation, or discrimination, on the other, as well as to realize that to the extent that we manage to escape the latter, we are automatically privileged. This does not mean that the sorrows caused by the challenges of ordinary life are not "real." But the heartache of losing a lover is hardly in the same category of suffering as the heartache of losing everyone you have ever loved to ethnic genocide. And all the traffic jams in the world cannot possibly match the injurious effects of social prejudice.

The very fact that some of us have the capacity to block out much of the world's violence is in itself a tremendous advantage; those of us who are able to lead lives that are not constantly focused on the utter fragility of human existence are fortunate. We may catch glimpses of this fragility during those moments when things don't work out for us—when other people or the world at large somehow disillusion us. But this cannot even begin to compare to the anxiety that arises from being forced to live under conditions that are consistently devastating. This less universal kind of vulnerability is precisely where Nietzsche's notion of loving one's fate starts to fall apart, for surely there is something preposterous, and even deeply alarming, about the idea that those struggling with drastic forms of circumstantial hardship should embrace their destinies; surely there is a limit to how much pain can productively be transformed into the raw materials of a better life. For one thing, those who have experienced more than their fair share of the world's hostility may find it difficult to trust this world, let alone see it as a space of possibility; even if the immediate source of trauma has vanished, it can be hard to feel safe. In this sense, one of the many tragedies of acute trauma is that it makes it harder for the traumatized person to take advantage of life's various opportunities. Keeping this understanding at the forefront of our consciousness should help us approach the universal vulnerabilities of human life with a degree of perspective, detachment, and even appreciation. If the everyday aggravations of living are the worst thing we have to deal with, then we really have very little to complain about.

3

Let me press the argument a step further by proposing that existential vulnerability—the kind of vulnerability that is foundational to human life rather than the result of oppressive circumstances—is actually a gift: our openness to the world may put us at risk, but it is also our lifeline in the sense that we can evolve only to the extent that we remain receptive to outside stimuli. For every external influence that disempowers us, there is another that augments us, adding layer upon layer of complexity to our character. This does not always mean that we become more refined, for promoting a distinctive character, as I have stressed, demands that we create room not only for what is pleasing and gracious, but also for what appears out of place, disorderly, unwieldy, and even a bit tumultuous or discomforting. But it does make us more multidimensional. From this point of view, the fact that our lives lack a fixed basis and a predetermined destiny can be deeply enlivening. After all, insofar as our lives are open-ended, they are also filled with possibility. And, in a way, the less we know about how they are supposed to transpire, the more leeway we have in shaping them.

Humans are distinctive among the creatures of the world in that we do not need to reconcile ourselves to any one incarnation of ourselves but have the capacity to reinvent ourselves an almost infinite number of times. We have the ability to take a step back and consider the entirety of our existence, including its purpose, as well as to revise whatever is not working about it. Best of all, we can do so repeatedly so that if our first attempt to improve the fit between our desires and our daily reality does not work, we can try again. Granted, it may be that few of us set about the task of fashioning a self in such a deliberate manner. Yet most of us have the potential to do so. Moreover, though we are historical beings in that we cannot have a sense of self without having a sense of our past, we are not even obliged to accept this past "as it comes" but possess the capacity to rewrite it from the perspective of the present. Among other things, we can reinterpret what was most difficult about the past as an indispensable component of our overall existential design, so that we, for instance, come to see that the childhood we experienced as excruciating is actually the foundation of our ability to relate to others with unusual sensitivity and compassion.

This is in part what Nietzsche is getting at with his notion of loving our fate: we accept that all the elements of the past that have gone into the making of who we are, the painful and the joyful alike, have contributed to our identity, so that if we disavow the painful elements, we also disavow vital aspects of our being. To love our fate means that we understand that we would not be who we are if we had not had our particular past. As a result, we no longer waste energy in trying to suppress key ingredients of our history but instead strive to "own" the sum total of this history by incorporating its variegated aspects into our distinctive art of living; no matter how distressing our past, we choose to appropriate it by making it a living component of our present. Because we cannot make the past go away, we turn it into something that is "necessary" for the actualization of our singularity. This is one way in which we manage to translate suffering into personal meaning. To be sure, this process may never be entirely successful. There may always be deposits of pain that remain beyond our reach—that we fail to integrate into the texture of our lives. But we can always make progress so that even if we cannot make the pain disappear, we can learn to live with it in such a way that it no longer has the power to dictate how we approach our current reality; we can acknowledge that the pain of the past will always be a part of the present without letting it determine the contours of this present.

4

This is not to say that the self we fashion will be either fully in control of itself or fully coherent. As I hope to have demonstrated, any particular incarnation of the self represents merely a partial (and always slightly faltering) crystallization of potentialities. Because all of us possess the raw materials for many different lives, because there are always many different versions of us that are competing to be lived, there are inevitably aspects of the self that are being sidelined in order to allow a specific identity to materialize. Because we are able to live only one of our possible lives at any given moment, we are obliged to marginalize a whole array of others; we are obliged to stifle components of our being that might be actualized by another set of existential choices. These marginalized components may be silenced, but they are never definitively banished, so that there is always the possibility that one of them starts to demand its due; there is always the chance that one of our "other" lives begins to ask for an audience. Consequently, any state of self-consistency we manage to attain is shaky at best. Because we are filled by unrealized potentialities as well as by various unconscious motivations that elude our command, our sense of being unitary creatures is always somewhat illusory. Yet this incompleteness comes with a benefit: it is exactly what allows us to craft ourselves afresh multiple times, always from a slightly different angle or starting point; it allows us to step into our art of living much more effectively than any permanent constellation of identity ever could.

On this account, the most "mature" self is not the one that is most sure of its boundaries, but rather one that is constantly able to rearrange these boundaries; the most "developed" self is not the one with the highest degree of structure, but rather one that is able to move flexibly between different dimensions of its identity, including those that are the least structured. This flexible movement is not always easy, for even if we are not born with a fixed self, we can over time acquire one that appears so: through repeated patterns of living, we can arrive at a self-definition that appears immutable because it is so deeply ingrained, so viscerally convincing to us, that it seems to convey the honest truth of our being. In other words, the fact that the self is open to construction and reconstruction does not mean that we do not experience its current version as binding. To the degree that we think of this version as who we really "are," it has tremendous power over what we can become, which is precisely why it would be useless to pretend that the past is not an active constituent of the present. Indeed, among the various constraints that limit our attempts at self-fashioning, none may be as powerful as the established editions of ourselves that we hold on to with a stubborn perseverance. And what is so ironic is that we often form such obstinate attachments to the most traumatized parts of our being, so that we tend to cling to our formative legacies of pain with an almost absurd doggedness.

I return to these concerns—including the legacies of pain—several times in the course of this book. For now, let me simply note that those with overly inflexible identities find ongoing self-poeticization difficult. In contrast, those who stay more agile remain capable of welding conflicting states of being into a livable reality, with the result that they also remain capable of fashioning themselves anew depending on the demands of the situation. This is not to suggest that we can survive without a degree of inner integration. Excessive fragmentation of our psychological and emotional organization would make our lives unmanageable, thwarting our ability to function in the world. Yet the more rigid our identities become, the more prone we are to symptomatic enactments, so that we, for example, repeat behavioral blueprints even when we know that these blueprints are not in the least bit productive. Although there may be some rigidities that hold value because they contain rich sediments of personal meaning—because they serve as important entry points to the specificity of our character—most impede our ability to enter into a nuanced relationship with our surroundings. And when these rigidities become overpowering, we lose touch with our lifelong occupation of crafting a character. We may even end up with a tyrannical version of the self that never allows competing versions their say. Such a tyrannical self displays a false coherence that diminishes our capacity for existential versatility even as it gives us the (mistaken) impression that we are in complete control of our destinies.[3]

5

When the center does not hold, we get lost and sometimes even fall ill. Yet if the center is too strong—if our inner organization is too seamless—we lose our suppleness and spontaneity. On this view, our "center" should never congeal into a static entity but should serve as a malleable mechanism for bringing together the various elements of our being. Ideally, this center should have a savvy (yet elastic and ever-evolving) intuition about the best ways to meet the world's myriad offerings. It should know not only what to embrace, but also what to exclude, for who we become depends as much on what we flee from as on what we let in. If it is true, as I have argued, that little contributes to our art of living more than the fact that we are asked to negotiate our identities in relation to what resides beyond us, it may well be that nothing is as important as recognizing which influences are worth nurturing and which are not. For instance, every relationship we form has the potential to change us, sometimes quite drastically. If there are people who awaken what is most interesting about us, there are others who can only diminish us. The latter rouse what is least generous, least noble and dignified about us, sending us into spirals of rage, jealousy, bitterness, covetousness, or mean-spiritedness. As a consequence, there is much to be said for being a little selective about whom we welcome into our lives.

To be sure, we are forced to interact with many people. From the woman who sells us our coffee in the morning to our colleagues, we are thrown into the company of others whom we may or may not appreciate. But when it comes to more intimate companions, such as friends and lovers, we have a great deal of say. We can surround ourselves with people who meet our needs and sometimes even make us aware of ones we did not know existed. Or we can select people who treat us badly, wound us, or make us feel small and insignificant. Because our patterns of relating are partially unconscious, it can admittedly be difficult to make good choices. Frequently we pick the wrong kinds of friends or lovers because we have not learned to select wisely. And it is not even necessarily the case that people who make us unhappy are invariably bad for us, for unhappiness often teaches us more than happiness. Yet fostering our ability to choose the right kinds of people can go a long way in sustaining our art of living.

Moreover, it is not only other people who mold our character, but also inanimate objects, cultural trends, works of art and entertainment, social belief systems and ideals, as well as the goals and ambitions we decide to pursue. The latter are particularly important, for in the same way that we invite certain kinds of people into our lives, we invite certain kinds of goals and ambitions into our universe, and these can have a tremendous influence on the general sketch of our lives. Some goals and ambitions lift us, whereas others are so uninspired that they render our lives mind-numbingly banal. This should give us some pause, for many of us go through life without giving our goals and ambitions much thought. Those that are most long-standing may be so habitual that we consider them more or less inevitable. Yet this inevitability is clearly not the case: it is always possible for us to change our goals and ambitions, and as we will see in the final section of this book, frequently this is exactly what those who respect the call of their character do, sometimes gradually, as a result of incremental revisions, other times quite suddenly, as if they were struck by lightning.

Generally speaking, one might say that the various things of the world—objects, beliefs, ideals, goals, ambitions, and other people, among many possibilities—actively summon us to our character. Whether we are talking about a book, film, or play that moves us, a news story or political speech that rouses our passions, a professional aspiration that motivates us to higher levels of performance, or a person who causes us to think differently, calls upon our empathy, or makes us madly in love, the details of the world leave a more or less pronounced mark on our identities. In addition, because the stream of influences we encounter is endless, our process of becoming is in principle also endless, coming to a conclusion only at death. Even the things that debilitate us—such as illnesses, accidents, and other misfortunes—bring something new to our lives, forcing us to adapt and reconfigure ourselves. We are used to thinking about this as a sign of decay, of losing important parts of ourselves. But if we understand human life as a process where process does not necessarily equal progress, even adversities that rob us of our strength or other faculties must be seen as crucial components of this process. It is not a matter of good or bad, positive or negative; it simply *is*. This process is what human life is made of, and there is no point in struggling against it.[4] But there is definitely a point to deciding how we are going to engage with it; there is a point to remaining alert to how we interact with the various stimuli directed at us.

6

In this context, it is helpful to keep in mind that if some aspects of the world summon us to our character, others distract us from it. In the same way that some people galvanize the best parts of our being, whereas others provoke the worst, some dimensions of our surroundings animate our character, whereas others deaden it, sometimes to the point of apathy. In other words, one of the dangers of our character-sculpting exposure to the world is that we can become flooded by its most conventional characteristics. We can unwittingly allow ourselves to be swept into patterns of appreciation— habits of endowing worth on some things but not on others— that are not of our own making, but that we have inherited from our families, teachers, friends, lovers, and culture at large. These patterns determine what we most cherish in our lives, yet there is absolutely no guarantee that they are appropriate for us. They may in fact damage our chances of finding our life's calling. They may convince us to adopt the values that are most readily available to us rather than to critically interrogate the system of values within which we operate. In this manner, we may become so invested in living the life that has been handed to us that we can no longer figure out what kind of life would actually satisfy us.

Our habitual social investments can thwart our ability to envision alternative ways of going about our lives. Such investments are seductive because they lend consistency to our existence by making it clear how we are supposed to behave. But they also constrict the field of possibility for us by downplaying some existential options while exaggerating the significance of others. This is in part why I have emphasized that it is all too easy to let the desires of our cultural environment engulf our own to such an extent that we no longer recognize the difference but assume that what we have been conditioned to want *is* in fact what we want; it is easy to become so thoroughly infested by conformist forms of desire that we direct our energies to certain sites of desirability—certain career choices, certain partners, certain cars, shoes, dishes, laptops, or vacations, and so on—merely because they are collectively recognized as desirable. Unfortunately, the more we do this, the more we lose track of the specificity of our desire and, therefore, of the distinctiveness of our character. We start to assess the overall "success" of our lives according to standards originating from outside of us, thereby becoming increasingly incapable of devising standards of our own.

Nothing is more tempting than going with the flow. Yet there are times when the only way to authentically respond to the call of our character is to wade against the current—when the desires that most accurately speak the language of our character are entirely different from those we have been accustomed to take for granted. In such situations, our task is to find our way out of the maze of collective desires that entrap us in complacent patterns of appreciation. Whether we are talking about our willingness to oppose an oppressive political system, our determination to defend a cause that seems doomed, or our ability to assert the singularity of our being over the predicates of social intelligibility that our cultural order insists on, we are expressing something about the almost inevitable clash between our social identity and our character. Although none of us can have patterns of appreciation that are completely divorced from the processes of socialization and cultural conditioning that have brought us into being, there is still a big difference between choosing a particular set of values because these values somehow resonate with us, on the one hand, and adopting this set because we are afraid to do otherwise, on the other. That is, when our choices arise from a fear of punishment rather than from an undercurrent of passion, we have sacrificed too much.

In the same way that our patterns of living over time give rise to an identity that feels entirely credible to us, the patterns of appreciation we grow up with can solidify into seemingly irrefutable belief systems even though there is nothing intrinsically "objective" about them. Although they are merely one very particular way of understanding the world (rather than a privileged expression of timeless truth), they can feel so utterly commonsensical that we cannot even imagine revising them. This is how social hegemonies function: we internalize cultural values on such a fundamental level that they begin to seem like self-evident "facts"; they come to possess an actuality that we no longer think to question. Even worse, we fault people from other cultures for being "barbaric" when they hold values that clash with ours even though their values appear just as indisputable to them as ours appear to us. Against this backdrop, listening to the call of our character is important not only because it facilitates our private process of self-actualization, but also because it is one of the few ways to ensure that we do not become so immersed in the values of our cultural order that we completely lose our critical faculties. It can serve as a means of defending the liveliness of our spirit, of fending off the kind of psychic death that can ensue from becoming too dedicated to collective norms that make us narrow-minded rather than inquisitive.

7

I want to be careful here. I am not saying that anything goes, that one set of cultural values is just as good as another. Although I believe that values are socially constructed rather than God given, I am not a strict relativist in the sense that I think that there are (or should be) universally applicable codes of conduct that, say, prevent discrimination. For instance, I do not believe that gender inequality is any more defensible than racial inequality, despite repeated efforts to pass it off as a culture-specific "custom" rather than an instance of injustice. There are many who disagree with me, and some of them are fellow academics who otherwise share a great deal with me. It can be difficult to prevent people from sliding from the idea that values are subjective to the idea that they all are equally desirable (or defensible). Yet I would insist that there are other ways to measure the desirability of values besides their supposed neutrality. One of these ways is the degree of violence perpetuated in the name of a specific value. There are of course different kinds of violence, so that it would be possible to assert that my insistence on gender equality violates the traditions of other cultures—that I am merely prolonging the legacies of Western colonialism by imposing my Western values on the rest of the world. But this objection gives the West too much credit by implying that gender equality is a specifically Western invention and, even more inaccurately, that Western women are free of discrimination. Women around the world are discriminated against—with greater and lesser degrees of explicitness—and I opt to uphold the ideal of getting rid of this discrimination because it seems like an ideal worth upholding. I do not need to claim that this choice is objective to claim that it is valid.[5]

I also want to avoid giving the impression that our cultural environment is invariably corrupting. As I hope to have made clear, we can develop an awareness of self only to the extent that we are embedded in the world, including the social world, so that it makes little sense to turn the world into some sort of a default adversary.[6] Our cultural environment is at once potentially enabling and potentially disabling, which is why one of the aims of this chapter has been to suggest that the best thing we can do for our character is to learn to make our way through the world's enticements with a degree of discrimination. Fortunately, as common as it is for us to give ourselves over to the wrong kinds of attractions, we usually know when we are doing so; we know when we are committing soul murder. Even at our most docile, we tend to recognize when we are entangled in existential scenarios that are not "meant" for us. As a consequence, even when we are living the most conventional life conceivable, the potential for rebelliousness, the potential for the spark of singularity, lies dormant within us.

This potential often leaps out when we least expect it. There are times when after a long period of conformity we suddenly find it impossible to go on as we always have—when we feel that a change of direction is essential for our survival.[7] We may not comprehend why the voice of our character breaks through in this way, but we definitely know when it does. During such moments, what is fierce and unapologetic about us ruptures our social facade, causing us to follow an inner directive that may be as enigmatic as it is compelling. This is how we sometimes come to make a U-turn in the middle of our lives—for example, by unexpectedly changing careers or dissolving a committed relationship. It is how we come to move to a new city, state, or country, leaving behind everything we know and love for the sake of an unknown future that inexplicably calls us. Our rational understanding that such sudden swerves of direction can cause mayhem not only in our own lives, but also in the lives of those close to us, does not usually keep them from seizing hold of our being in ways that make them hard to resist.

Although I am certainly not advocating selfish actions that hurt others, I think that it would be a mistake to ignore the times when our character clamors for recognition in this manner. At the very least, it deserves a careful hearing, even if we in the end decide to decline its invitation. Sometimes there is a specific trigger: experiencing the death of someone close to us, being abandoned by a lover, being laid off from work, failing to attain an important goal, getting disappointing news, and so on. There may, in other words, be a life-altering epiphany that makes us feel that the life we have been living is no longer livable. Other times, a long-standing discontent finally steals upon us so that we know that things have to change in order for us to be able to go on. Either way, we come to view the world or some facet of our lives from a perspective that was not previously available to us; we come to see aspects of our reality that have hitherto remained invisible. When this happens on the collective level, it can generate a political crisis or even a revolution. On the personal level, it prompts us to make radical modifications to our lives regardless of what this costs us, so that we may suddenly find ourselves dropping old goals and ambitions and pursuing new ones that we might have earlier found completely inconceivable.

I come back to such turning points in chapter 7. At this junction, it is enough to observe that there is often a lack of moderation to our character that stuns our social persona. This is exactly why it has the power to dislodge us from the "reasonable" composition of our everyday experience. It is why one of the biggest challenges of human existence is to be able to respond to the call of our character without at the same time wrecking the rest of our lives. I stress this point because even though I am clearly rooting for what is singular rather than sanitized, I would never want to imply that our character should always trump our social or interpersonal commitments. Ideally, we should be able to feel authentic while simultaneously participating in the social activities, obligations, and responsibilities that bring stability to our lives. The rest of this book offers various suggestions on how best to accomplish this. But at the root of the matter resides the idea I have been developing this far—namely, that the self is an open system that is always in the process of becoming, of fashioning its distinctive art of living, and even, in some instances, of claiming the right to be the (ever-tentative and sometimes highly experimental) poet of its experience. As I have specified, there is no such thing as a fully realized self. There are only repeated efforts to step into the turbulent stream of life in ways that allow for increasing levels of psychological and emotional acumen. Those who admit this find it easier to let one aspect of the self speak without thereby suppressing its other aspects, with the consequence that they may also be able to cultivate their character without ravaging their social viability.

3

The Specificity of Desire

The object is by nature a refound object.
—Jacques Lacan

1

Let us take a closer look at the idea that we are never fully self-actualized and in particular the idea that our sense of deprivation—our sense of being perpetually "unfinished"—is not an impediment to an inspired life, but rather its precondition. This is a bold claim, for it aligns inspiration with lack, with what philosophers such as Sartre have characterized as the "nothingness" that punctures our "being."[1] In the final chapters of this book, I explain why this alignment is not always accurate, why some of our most inspired moments are ones when we feel utterly complete. I am, in other words, by no means saying that deprivation is the only way to attain inspiration. Richness often begets more richness, abundance more abundance. There are times when we invent wonderful things, such as art, love, beauty, values, ideals, or

beliefs, for the simple reason that we need a way to consume a surplus of creative impulses that would otherwise feel unmanageable.
During such times, our energies overflow, forging new pathways as
well as building unanticipated connections between already existing pathways, thereby allowing us to rearrange the coordinates of
our existence. This capacity to mold conduits of energy into novel
configurations represents an important facet of creativity—one
that is predicated on the pressure of fullness rather than of lack,
so that the more saturated, the more crowded with stimuli we feel,
the more easily we are able to bring new things into being.

But I do also believe that there is a strong link between our
sense of lack (emptiness or inner dissatisfaction) and creativity.
This is because lack gives rise to desire. It makes us want things,
and sometimes the best way to get these things is to invent them.
Alternatively, we can scour the world for already existing things
that might satisfy us. Either way, we are motivated by the urge to
fill the lack within our being: in the same way that an empty room
invites us to furnish it, our inner nothingness invites us to populate
it with things that mean something to us.

I am using the word *thing* quite freely here, for it can refer to
anything from material objects to personal values to other people.
In a sense, it hardly matters what we stuff into the void of our
being as long as we are able to alleviate the anxiety this void tends
to generate. In another sense, however, nothing is as important as
the quality of the things we either invent or discover, for—as I suggested in the previous chapter—it is when we fail to pay attention
to the specific texture of the things we reach for that we tend to
clutter our inner world, not to mention our daily lives, with things
that do not bring us any real satisfaction and that might even
harm our chances of finding personal meaning. Sadly, our desperate quest for meaning (or self-fulfillment) can sometimes drive us
to accumulate heaps of irrelevant things that we do not need and
that burden us by their sheer excess; ironically, the very things we
resort to in order to ward off the nothingness that threatens to
engulf us can in turn engulf us. This is how we come to spawn a
great deal of waste. Our collective efforts to flee from our lack have

created societies drowning in litter and other useless items, so that we spend considerable resources managing the residue of our avarice.

I have already noted the hoarding mentality that sometimes gets the better of us: the fact that no matter how much we have, we tend to want more. Such excess of hunger can be a response to an excess of emptiness—a futile attempt to comfort the hollow place within us that weeps even when we smile. Most problematically, when this hunger gets intertwined with more circumstantial forms of hunger, such as the desperation to beat the odds of poverty, it can fuel what cultural critic Lauren Berlant calls "cruel optimism": the unfounded faith that one's tireless efforts to find material success, cultural acceptance, or everyday stability will eventually pay off no matter how bleak one's situation. Berlant focuses specifically on how socially marginalized individuals often continue to make emotional investments in the very collective structures and belief systems—say, the ideals of liberal capitalism—that oppress them in the first place. Such is the predicament, for instance, of the working-class adolescent who has watched his or her parents toil without reward for two decades, but who still believes that hard work will automatically result in class mobility and social belonging.[2] My emphasis here is more on the false optimism of those who assume that amassing an enormous pile of material resources will somehow shield them from the realization that it is our plight as human beings to live with a degree of deprivation, that, ontologically speaking, we will never be (or have) "enough." But both scenarios highlight the ways in which lack can give rise to misguided exertions to overcome it.

The difference, of course, is that the kind of circumstantial lack Berlant is talking about could be rectified by a more egalitarian socioeconomic order. It is hard to tolerate in part because it is in principle unnecessary; it is not an essential part of the human condition, but rather the outcome of a deficient political organization. And, on the practical level, it is also hard to tolerate because there are few effective ways to compensate for it. In contrast, the kind of foundational (ontological) lack I am analyzing can be countered by a whole host of constructive undertakings. Although it can certainly breed the sort of surplus of greed I have sought to problematize, we also possess quite a few innovative means of coping with it. Indeed, our unease in the face of this lack has arguably produced many of the most prized objects and activities of human history: from books, paintings, sculptures, photographs, and love poems to philosophies of living, scientific discoveries, ethical systems, exploratory expeditions, and working fireplaces—noble things have arisen from our sense of dispossession. This is why it is possible to argue that our foundational lack holds tremendous value even when we acknowledge that our circumstantial deprivation rarely leads to the good life that we are programmed to fantasize about. In the same way that our foundational vulnerability is not merely what injures us, but also what makes us receptive to the world's enabling influences, our foundational lack opens to realms of creativity without which our lives would be much less captivating.

2

To understand the connection between lack and creativity, it may help to think about it in concrete terms. Consider what happens when we lose a person we love. The void left by this person may initially be so devastating that we cannot find a way to go on with our lives. Our grief slows down our private universe, sometimes to the point of paralysis. This is a necessary part of mourning and frequently quite productive because it forces us to take notice of aspects of our being that we usually ignore. There may be reticent voices within us that cannot normally fight their way into our consciousness because the noisier, more insistent ones take up so much space. Grief has a way of making such tenuous voices audible; it stills the habitual commotion of our interiority so that we can gain access to new layers of self-awareness. Yet as long as we remain within the crypt of our sadness, we cannot usually reap the benefits of our deepened self-understanding; we cannot take advantage of our increased wisdom until we have started to loosen the grip of mourning. And nothing signals our capacity to do so better than our ability to creatively reach for a suitable substitute for what we have lost.

The time of grief can feel endless. But, eventually, the void caused by our loss asks to be filled; it drives us to look for replacements. Sometimes this means finding another person to love. Other times it means finding another way to gain satisfaction so that we, for instance, pour our energies into a creative project, an intellectual exertion, a professional goal, or a political ambition. Happily for us, we do not need to find an exact duplicate of the person we have lost, but merely someone (or something) capable of engaging our passion as powerfully. Similarly, the best way to get over a disappointed aspiration is to counter it with a new one that absorbs us as thoroughly as the one we were unable to bring to fruition. The minute our desire invents or discovers a new object—the minute we find ourselves connecting with a new person or aspiration—we have taken the first step toward overcoming our sadness; we have begun to gradually give up what we once held dear so that something different can become equally valuable to us.

One reason this process can be so agonizing is that it is intrinsically paradoxical: it recognizes the value of the old, often to the point of worship, while slowly working toward the new. But there is no denying that the moment the new becomes a real possibility, the moment we manage to envision a genuinely viable alternative to what we have lost, is the moment when the present begins to eclipse the past. This transition of course does not necessarily erase our ambivalence about our loss, let alone our faithfulness to what we have lost. There may be key losses in our lives—losses of people or aspirations that feel absolutely irreplaceable—that we might never be able to surpass entirely. Such people or aspirations may leave an enduring imprint on our psyches, becoming a more or less prominent ingredient of our overall inner composition. One might in fact say that to the extent that our psyches hold the (conscious or unconscious) memory of everything we have lost, our identities cannot be divorced from the people and aspirations we have left behind; our personalities always carry the nostalgic trace of our losses. Yet if we are to go on with our lives, if we are to

invent or discover new sources of passion, eventually we will need
to break the paralysis of grief; we will need to find new objects
for our desire even when we cannot quite banish the ghosts of the
old ones.[3]

The acute void left by the loss of a loved person or aspiration is
not the same thing as the ubiquitous existential malaise (or foundational lack) I have started to align with creativity. But the principle is the same—namely, that our lack gives rise to an impulse to
invent or discover entities that are capable of granting us a compensatory satisfaction. Simply put, our sense that something is
missing from our lives spurs us to imaginative activity, inciting us,
as it were, to play with nothingness. According to this account,
many of the most valuable things in life result from the fact that
we are never fully adjusted to our environment—that our interactions with the world tend to leave us slightly disgruntled. As I have
pointed out, if we felt entirely fulfilled, we would quickly lose our
motivation for invention and discovery; our self-sufficiency would
kill our curiosity about the world. Consequently, although we
may fantasize about the possibility of absolute happiness, about a
seamless fit between us and the world, the fact that we are unable
to achieve this fantasy is the source of a great deal of magnificence.

3

We have, once again, arrived at the idea that the world is a source
of both wonder and frustration. I began this chapter with a quota-
tion from Jacques Lacan because there are few thinkers who have
articulated this tension more persuasively. Lacan explains that our
relationship to the world is inherently conflicted. On the one hand,
we can attain a fully human existence only by inserting ourselves
into preexisting structures of language and collective meaning. If we
refused to do so, or if we were somehow incapable of accomplishing this task, we would not develop the capacity to speak, relate,
love, or make meaning; we would be trapped in a solipsistic bubble
that would make it impossible for us to gain either psychological

or emotional depth. This is why processes of socialization are indispensable for human intelligibility, why, as I have stressed, we cannot accurately describe human life without describing our radical dependence on others. This is essentially the same thing as saying that we would be nothing without the world: we draw our power, our resources, from the power and resources of the world.

On the other hand, our reliance on the world can be humbling. Precisely because we can survive only through participating in collective, impersonal systems of meaning and value, we come to recognize our relative insignificance; we come to see that we are merely a tiny element of the world's overall organization. We cannot, for instance, usually amend a cultural belief or practice without eliciting the assistance of others; no matter how outdated this belief or practice may be, and no matter how exasperated it may make us, we do not have the power to revise it without turning to others for help. There are of course exceptions to this predicament. There are writers whose prose becomes so influential that it alters cultural views or standards of artistic excellence. There are painters, composers, photographers, and other creative individuals whose work causes dramatic shifts in their respective fields. There are scientists, inventors, politicians, and lawmakers whose contributions to society enhance the lived reality of all of us. And there are courageous activists whose fervor for change actually manages to bring about such change: there are individuals whose voices are so charismatic that we have no choice but to pay attention. But most of us do not ever attain this level. And even those who do attain it don't usually experience themselves as omnipotent; even the most gifted among us are prone to the dissatisfaction that stems from feeling that no matter what we do, it is never quite enough. If anything, the more ambitious the aspiration, the more likely it is that the person trying to attain it feels inadequate to the task.

Lacan posits that our sense of inadequacy is primordial—and thus impossible to banish—because it is the price we pay for socialization. Prior to socialization, we do not yet understand ourselves as separate entities, which in practice means that we are the world and the world is us. Socialization shatters this illusion at least on two different levels. On a literal level, it introduces a wedge—an insurmountable obstacle—between us and the maternal body (or the body of the one who cares for us). On a more figurative level, it delivers a huge blow to our narcissistic sense of being the navel of the universe. In so doing, it divests us of our infantile fantasy of wholeness and uncomplicated belonging, generating an unquenchable longing for a state of plenitude that we imagine we have somehow been unfairly robbed of: a lost paradise we can never recover but that we spend the rest of our lives pursuing. The fact that we never possessed this paradise in the first place, that we were never completely whole and at ease to begin with, does not in the least diminish our resolve to recover it. Lacan designates this lost paradise as "the Thing," indicating by the capital T that it is not an ordinary fantasy object, but a very special Thing of incomparable worth; it is the Thing that our deepest desires are made of.[4]

Some of us replace the lost paradise that the Thing symbolizes with an otherworldly paradise, which is arguably one reason religion wields so much power around the globe. But many of us go about the undertaking in the way I have outlined—namely, by finding surrogates for what we think we have lost: we pursue people and various aspirations to alleviate the ache within our being. This is why Lacan asserts that "the object is by nature a refound object."[5] Every "object" (every person or aspiration) we invent or discover is "refound" in the sense that it is always a substitute for the original lost Thing. We place one thing, one object, after another into the empty slot left by the Thing, and those objects that come the closest to reviving the Thing, that contain the strongest echo of the Thing's special radiance, are the ones we feel most passionate about. However, because no object can ever fully replicate the fantasized perfection of the Thing, we are condemned to repeat our quest ad infinitum. We are, so to speak, always on the lookout for the perfect object that would, once and for all, grant us the unmitigated satisfaction we (fantasmatically) associate with the missing Thing. This is why we spend our lives concocting ever more ingenious ways of resurrecting it. One might in fact go as far as to say that it is because we do not have the Thing that the various things of the world matter to us in the first place; it is because we feel deprived of the Thing that we are capable of being interested in (and devoted to) things other than ourselves.

I have proposed that it is because we cannot locate the ultimate meaning of our lives that we are compelled to produce more partial meanings that resonate with the uniqueness of our character. Similarly, it is because we cannot have the Thing that we feel motivated to reach for its echo through the various objects that we encounter in the world; it is because we cannot have the sublime object that we are driven to look for its luster in more mundane substitutes. Such substitutes may fall short of the Thing's luminescence, yet insofar as they evoke it, they lend meaning to our lives. As to which objects speak to us and which do not, that is determined by the always highly idiosyncratic manner in which we experience the Thing's absence. In other words, the specificity of our desire—what Lacan calls the "truth" of our desire—has to do with the unique parameters of our sense of existential deprivation.

Note, once more, how fortunate it is that the objects we invent or discover as deputies for the Thing do not need to—indeed, cannot—ever reincarnate it flawlessly, for if they were to do so, our creative impulse would come to a halt. It is because the things of the world do not necessarily bear any obvious resemblance to the Thing that human creativity can take so many different forms; the gap between the Thing and the things we use to compensate for its absence guarantees that there is room for innovation. Without this gap, we—as well as the societies in which we live—would languish, for there would be no incentive to keep devising new modalities of meaning and value. Established meanings and values would become so entrenched that they would be totalitarian. On this view, the lack within our being is the foundation not only of our personal transformation, but also—insofar as a large enough accumulation of personal transformations results in cultural transformation—of the advancement of society.

4

Regrettably, there are times when we lose track of the fact that the correspondence between the lost Thing and the things we turn to as its representatives does not need to be entirely accurate; there are times when we ravage the integrity of our objects by trying to force them to coincide with our fantasy of what we have lost. This is one reason it might be a good idea to heed the advice of Heidegger, who urges us to allow the things of the world to disclose themselves to us according to their own distinctive rhythm;[6] it is why it might sometimes be wise to take a step back from the world so as to create space for objects to materialize in their own way, without any interference from us. This is perhaps nowhere as important as in our relationships with other people and particularly with those we love, for our temptation to use them as a means of plugging the void within our being can cause us to conflate them with the fantasy object (the Thing) to such an extent that we fail to respect their independent reality. In such cases, our affection is narcissistic rather than generous in the sense that its goal is to make us feel better about ourselves rather than to pay tribute to the singularity of the other person; it is essentially selfish in that what we are looking for is a solution to our own sense of incompleteness rather than a genuine connection to another person.

Such a narcissistic attitude can be hard to sidestep in the context of romance because the Thing is never as powerful, as likely to exhilarate us, as it is when we fall in love. Though we have the capacity to raise more or less any object to the Thing's special status, nothing invites us to do so more ardently (or explicitly) than the object of our love. The person we love seems to contain a living and breathing morsel of the Thing, which is why we are prone to idealize (and even overidealize) him or her. And inasmuch as our object gives us the impression that we can touch the Thing in tangible ways that make unmediated satisfaction available to us, it can be virtually impossible to resist; it is because the love object promises the end of alienation that our desire solidifies around it with extraordinary intensity. Within this heady state, it is all too easy to fall into a narcissistic fixation that causes us to treat our beloved as a mere instrument of our own salvation.

It is, then, possible to develop a mercenary attitude toward our loved ones. Indeed, ironically enough, it is when we pursue the fullness of our own experience most determinedly that we are most likely to ignore the multidimensionality of those close to us, with the result that we see in them only what we want to see and value only those of their attributes that appear to seal the lack within our being. In such situations, we sideline, and sometimes even resent, those dimensions of others that do not cater to our needs, thereby developing a one-sided understanding of who they are. We studiously avoid those of their characteristics that confuse the fantasmatic image we hold of them, privileging instead what makes sense to us from our self-serving perspective. In this way, even the luster of the Thing we locate in another person—the sublime echo of special significance that renders a given individual unfathomably precious to us—can become abusive when it overshadows the rest of this person's character. When this luster becomes the only thing we appreciate about another person, we may have attained our ideal, but we have lost the person.

Narcissism is the very opposite of authentic relationality, for whenever we operate from a narcissistic premise, we cannot really see the other person, but rather bask in the flattering image of ourselves that he or she reflects back to us. In addition, because it is not possible for anyone to uphold this image entirely reliably—because components of a given person's own character will sooner or later cloud its clarity—we are bound to be disappointed. Insofar as we are looking for what another person can never grant us, namely a version of ourselves that is more complete than what we are able to attain on our own, every person is fated to let us down. Even a person who contains an unusually strong echo of the Thing, who resonates on the precise frequency of our desire, cannot do so consistently. Because even the most enthralling person is never *merely* this echo—because every person exceeds the specifications of our desire in countless different ways—we can never find a person who will invariably satisfy us.

From this viewpoint, we make a mistake when we collapse the distinction between self and other and reduce the other to the coordinates of our desire. This is why it is essential to recognize that no matter how much pleasure others give us, they cannot deliver us from our existential malaise. They cannot heal our wounds, make us whole, conjure away our pain, or complete us in any definitive sense. They may offer us moments of self-actualization; but they cannot give us redemption.

5

This is not to deny that there are objects that approximate the Thing more loyally than others. Such objects enchant us more than those where the Thing's echo remains more subdued or diffuse; they transmit something about the Thing's original splendor, so that when we are in their presence, we feel more elevated, more self-realized, than when we are forced to function in a universe of less venerable substitutes. It is as if, to once again borrow from Lacan, they contained something "more than" themselves, so that when we interact with them, we interact with both the objects themselves and the trace of the Thing that these objects hold.[7] This is why we value some objects over others, some people and aspirations over others. Our appreciation can in fact become nearly obsessive, so that we cannot bear the thought of losing those objects that most robustly communicate the Thing's majesty. Such objects wield an enormous amount of power over us, for they promise unadulterated fulfillment, with the consequence that we cannot even imagine giving them up. And when we lose such an object, our grief is greater than what we experience in the aftermath of more ordinary objects.

This clarifies a great deal about the specificity of human desire. On the one hand, it is true—as I have explained—that we are astonishingly versatile when it comes to finding ways to compensate for our lack. We can get our satisfaction from a variety of different sources so that some of us, for example, value relationships over all other things, whereas others assess work or creative endeavors to be so rewarding that they consistently opt for them at the expense of relationships. And most of us operate within a complex field of investments so that one moment we devote our energies to our relationships, another to our careers, and yet another to a book, a hobby, a solitary walk, or a slice of blueberry pie. On the other hand, we tend to be quite discriminating about the investments we make. It is simply not the case that any slice of blueberry pie will do. There is a flexibility about the sources of our pleasure, but within each "category" of pleasure (relationships, careers, books, etc.), there is a hierarchy among the components so that one activity with our friends will fulfill us more than another, one career triumph will be sweeter than another, one book will engross us more than another, and so on. Moreover, even if two people like the same book, their appreciation is unlikely to manifest in the same way. Because the echo of the Thing reverberates differently for each of us, no two people's desires are exactly the same.

This specificity of desire is one of the major causes of our suffering, for more often than not, we cannot quite get what we want. It can be tricky to find the right kinds of objects, so that we can, for instance, go for long periods without a romantic relationship because we do not come across anyone who matches the frequency of our desire. Even when we interact with countless people who in principle meet all the necessary specifications of desirability, we cannot force ourselves to want any of them if they fail to emit a strong enough echo of the Thing. The flipside of this is that when we do locate the right person, it can be very difficult for us to shift our desire to another even when the person in question is not available or rejects us. In addition—and this point bears repeating—when we lose such a person or his or her love, we are much more devastated than when we lose someone who has merely scratched the surface of our affections. Along closely related lines, when we (due to an accident, illness, or old age, for example) become incapable of pursuing an aspiration that has given us uncommon pleasure, we might find it harder to adjust to the loss than we would with some less meaningful activity.

Even though we possess innumerable options for coping with our inner void, finding just the right approach can be challenging. And one of the thorniest things about life are those moments when the object we have settled on does not alleviate our lack but instead adds sting to it by disillusioning us—as is the case, for instance, when someone we love humiliates us. When a fresh lack meets the original lack we are trying to redress, we can be mortified beyond expression. In such instances, there is too much of lack, as it were, so that we feel defeated by the sheer vastness of our deprivation. Our wound is so gaping that we cannot even begin to imagine how we might fill it. This is one way we arrive at depression. Alternatively, we may succumb to addictions, using work, sex, food, drugs, alcohol, or even self-inflicted pain as a coping mechanism. We operate under the erroneous impression that the more work, sex, food, or anything else we cram into the void within our being, the fuller we will feel. And our disappointment about the outcome only reinforces the cycle, so that the less satisfied we feel, the more relentlessly we seek satisfaction. This is one reason addictions are so difficult to break. The only way out of the rotation is to be willing to tolerate the pain that arises from lack, and many of us are not that strong. Or at least we are not *always* that strong.

The specificity of our desire can thus cause us a great deal of trouble. But this difficulty does not change the fact that our ability to find the echo of the Thing in ordinary objects—as Lacan puts it, to endow mundane things with "the dignity of the Thing"[8]—is our best line of defense against our encroaching sense of nothingness. Although there is no ultimate cure for this nothingness, many of us manage to lead relatively satisfied lives through the kinds of compensatory measures I have delineated. As long as we have access to objects and activities that engage our passion, we are to some extent inoculated against the anxiety caused by our lack. To be sure, this lack will always lurk in the shadows of our interiority, waiting for those moments when we, for one reason or another, fail to find a suitable object or activity. During such moments, our lack will slide into the forefront of our consciousness, rendering us acutely aware of our vulnerability. If we are lucky, such moments will pass quickly so that we can, once again, focus on things that confer meaning to our lives. In this sense, our pursuit of personal meaning—of a life that feels worth living—is an attempt to send our lack back into its hiding place. And because this is never a permanent solution, because, as I have maintained, we can never pinpoint a meaning that will forever release us from our lack, we have no choice but to repeatedly renew our pursuit; we have no choice but to endlessly resuscitate our desire to make meaning out of the raw ingredients we have been given (or chance upon in the world).

6

I have shown that one of the many ruses of social power is to silence the specificity of our desire and to replace it with purely conventional yearnings. Against this backdrop, what is so miraculous about the Thing's echo is that it tends to trump such yearnings. Precisely because it expresses something about the utterly distinctive manner in which each of us experiences our existential deprivation, it cannot easily be reconditioned to follow cultural (general rather than specific) scripts. Consequently, whenever the Thing's echo resounds strongly enough in an object (person or aspiration) we have selected, it overpowers the social voices telling us that we have made a bad choice. For example, our cultural environment may try to convince us that we have fallen in love with a person of the "wrong" age, race, gender, ethnicity, religion, social class, or educational level. Our family, relatives, friends, and former lovers may inform us that our partner is not suitable for us. Alternatively, those around us may attempt to talk us out of taking a specific job because (they think) it will make us miserable: it is too ambitious, too stressful, too demanding, too this or that. But once our desire has been fully engaged, such warnings have little power. Even when we rationally admit that the voices that surround us have a point, we cannot keep ourselves from seeing our lover or taking that job. This is because the echo of the Thing is more compelling than reason.

One might say that the Thing's echo introduces a code of ethics that is drastically different from the one that dictates the parameters of socially legitimate longings. Although there is no doubt that our desire can become so specific, so rigidly fixed, as to be pathological (more on this in the next chapter), there is also a certain integrity to its specificity—an integrity that makes us courageous enough to stand up for ourselves when our environment tells us that our desire is injudicious. In fact, inasmuch as this integrity makes it possible for us to perceive the preciousness of what we are socially encouraged to shun, ignore, or trivialize, it allows us to make room for values that are not culturally valued, ideals that are not culturally idealized, and meanings that are not culturally recognized as meaningful. It, potentially at least, empowers us to devise patterns of appreciation that deviate from the ones we have been conditioned to uphold, thereby translating desires that are normatively considered devoid of worth into something profoundly (and personally) worthwhile.[9] This is why our ability to revere the Thing's echo is, for Lacan, not only what satisfies us on an individual level, but also a binding ethical imperative—why he famously posits that "ceding on" the truth of our desire is an ethical failure of tremendous proportions.[10]

Lacan implies that our loyalty to the Thing's echo protects us against the nihilistic tendency to think that no matter how much we strive to formulate new values, ideals, meanings, and patterns of appreciation, the social establishment will always defeat us. Because the Thing's distinctive code of ethics gives us pause whenever we are asked to betray the truth of our desire, it safeguards us against complete social capture. This is an ethics that is not dictated by the instrumentalist imperatives of utility but rather assesses the value of objects—as well as of the ethical actions related to these objects—on the basis of their proximity (or faithfulness) to the Thing. The object that comes the closest (or remains the most faithful) to the Thing is, ethically speaking, more important than one that is merely useful. As a result, if ethics in its usual sense deliberates on the prudence or imprudence (or, more nobly, on the rightness or wrongness) of this or that action, Lacanian ethics is a matter of pursuing the echo of the Thing regardless of social cost; it is a matter of following our passion—the distinctive thread of our desire—even when doing so means going against the morality of the dominant cultural order. This is why Lacan boldly states that the "only thing of which one can be guilty of is having given ground relative to one's desire."[11]

This is obviously a complicated ethical stance in that there may be situations where our desire is not particularly palatable or where it conflicts with the desires of others.[12] Yet Lacan's vision is not meant as a call to selfishness, but rather as an urgent reminder that some paths of desire are more truthful—and more singularizing—than others. People who complain about a general sense of apathy often do so because they have lost touch with the Thing's echo; they have lost their capacity to distinguish between objects that correspond to the inimitable intonation of their desire and others that merely grant the illusion of satisfaction. One reason for this is that the vast commercial machinery of our society is explicitly designed to drown out the Thing's echo. This machinery makes so many sparkly decoys available to us that we can get sidetracked by the huge volume of our choices. Such decoys, which press on us from all sides, obscure the Thing's aura for the simple reason that they are deliberately manufactured to shine extra brightly. They flood us with a homogenizing blare that can induce us to accumulate the piles of useless junk I referred to earlier. The materialism of the Western world has in fact reached embarrassing proportions, so that the number of alluring distractions vying for our attention in an average department store or suburban mall can be overwhelming, as can the variety of things that flash across our television screens on a nightly basis. And the fact that the West's affluence has often been purchased at the expense of less privileged societies only adds exigency to the necessity of resuscitating the Thing's ethical code—a code that makes us more selective (and thus less wasteful) in relation to the world's offerings.

In our culture, it is easy to attribute the Thing's aura to too many objects, so that we mistake the decoy for the genuine article. Fortunately, though, the opposite usually does not happen: we rarely hesitate in the face of the genuine article. That is, we usually know when we have stumbled upon the "real" thing;[13] we know immediately when we have come across an object that matches the stipulations of our desire. In this sense, recognizing the right object is not the hard part. What takes so much effort is learning to dodge the lures that misdirect our desire by offering a plausible masquerade of the Thing's echo. Obviously, the more connected we remain to the specificity of our desire, the less likely it is that we will be seduced by the masquerade. Furthermore, to the degree that we consistently choose well, we build an ever-expanding repertoire of memories that contribute to the gradual elaboration of our character. The objects that compose this repertoire become consequential beyond their time-specific "use value." We endow them with an enduring significance because they contain a sedimented record of our history. On this view, our faithfulness to the Thing is not merely a matter of discovering its echo in different objects over time, but also of sustaining our ability to discover it repeatedly in the same object; it is a matter of finding ever new ways of appreciating our most treasured objects.

7

In this context, it is useful to recognize that we have been granted one particularly effective tool for resurrecting the Thing's echo: language. According to the account I have given, we revive the dignity of the Thing when we, for instance, fall in love or invest ourselves in an important personal aspiration. In comparison, the powers of language may seem feeble. Yet there is perhaps nothing in our lives that allows us to access the Thing's echo as dependably as language. Though on the one hand language is a big part of the very socialization process that seems to deprive us of the Thing to begin with, on the other it offers us a dexterous means of dealing with our dispossession. Among other things, it is a versatile medium for introducing new values, ideals, meanings, and patterns of appreciation into the world. In addition, even creative endeavors that do not rely on language, such as painting, sculpture, photography, and dance, can be enriched by an encounter with language. In other words, the reward we get from a painting (to take just one example) can be multiplied by our ability to attribute various meanings to it, so that as much pleasure has arisen from our efforts to decipher Mona Lisa's smile as from the smile itself.

Although there may be experiences, such as erotic or meditative states, that are diluted by the intrusion of language, most products of human activity profit from the layers of language that accumulate around them. An ancient play or poem (already a linguistic artifact) gathers weightiness from the interpretations that generations of readers have placed on it. This is why there is something uniquely delicious about reading a musty, fraying volume that countless other readers have handled and marked; the scribblings on the margins, along with the less tangible associations circulating in our culture, can be valuable additions to the original text rather than something that mars its purity. Similarly, what people have over the years made of certain politicocultural interventions is as much a part of our heritage as those interventions themselves. The reams of writing produced by something like the Declaration of Independence or Martin Luther King Jr.'s "I Have a Dream" speech, though perhaps not as important as the declaration or the speech itself, play a central part in our collective history.

What is more, although it is certainly possible to become addicted to words in the same way that we can become addicted to many other things, this is not usually a calamity. Verbosity can be annoying to others, and there may even be cases where the inability to stop speaking or writing exhausts us, but speaking or writing does not generally damage us (unless of course we choose to speak or write against social hegemonies that have the power to take revenge on us). That is, language is usually a fairly benign "solution" to the gnawing lack within our being, provided we do not let it degenerate into meaningless chatter. And, from a slightly different perspective, it can even help those who have in one way or another been traumatized. It is not a coincidence that trauma survivors often feel an overwhelming need to tell their stories, for there can be something cathartic about capturing the painful event within a network of words. When trauma is translated into language, words become a barrier of sorts between the traumatic experience and the person who has undergone this experience; they function as a distancing mechanism that creates some space between the trials of the past and the present moment, thereby making it less likely that the survivor will relive the traumatizing experience indefinitely.

This is not to say that the narrativization of trauma is effortless. One of the most common responses to extreme suffering is silence. And for some individuals, silence may even be a way of working through their suffering. Yet for many others, the (repeated) telling of hurtful experiences is the first step toward being able let go of some of their pain. This is the principle behind most Western therapeutic approaches. And it is also what underpins personal or collective efforts to convert pain into words. These efforts may consist of something as simple as a personal journal or they may produce something as sophisticated as an autobiographical novel. Alternatively, they may take the form of a poem, a song, or a magazine article. Other times, they may result in a political rally or a religious gathering. Such personal or collective attempts to communicate pain and to witness the pain of others return a modicum of agency to survivors. Even though they rarely produce a triumphant overcoming—even though trauma's impact tends to linger far beyond such interventions—they do often offer some relief. It is as if they provided a secure place to lean on so that it becomes possible for survivors to relinquish some of their self-protective (but exhausting) guardedness in relation to the world.

The foundational lack I have been discussing in this chapter is not the same thing as the pain of acute trauma. Like the existential vulnerability I spoke about in the previous chapter, the lack I have been analyzing here is more universal, more equally distributed, than trauma. But the insight about the power of language is equally applicable in the sense that language may well be our strongest shield against the demons of emptiness. In the context of severe trauma, there may be other things that are more effective, such as justice or retribution; a sense of closure may in many instances do more than the ability to give an account of our experiences. But when it comes to our foundational lack, there is no possibility of justice or retribution; there is no closure, unless one considers death as one. Fortunately for us, language thrives on this open-endedness, so that there is in principle no limit to our ability to use constellations of language to throw a protective cloak over our lack. Such constellations can be poetic or metaphoric, as is usually the case with art, or they can be highly functional, as is the case with the language of science and everyday pragmatism. Either way, they place a veil of sorts between us and our lack so that we do not need to experience the immensity of our emptiness; they render our malaise less immediate, less insistent, so that it cannot consistently derail us. In this sense, although it may well be that without language—which is, among other things, an instrument of consciousness—we might not have an awareness of our inner lack in the first place, language is also one of our best antidotes to this lack.

PART II

THE ART OF
SELF-RESPONSIBILITY

4

The Blueprints of Behavior

The manifestations of a compulsion to repeat . . . give the appearance of some "daemonic" force at work.

—Sigmund Freud

1

One of Freud's most influential findings was the so-called repetition compulsion: the idea that we tend to repeat blueprints of behavior that are not good for us.[1] This is the case when we, despite our earnest efforts to the contrary, fall into the same relationship problems, the same professional dilemmas, the same maddening "issues" with our partners, parents, siblings, friends, or coworkers, as we always have. We may find ourselves regularly attracted to lovers who disillusion us. We may find ourselves endlessly replicating the same professional failures. Or we may find ourselves fighting with our father in exactly the same way as we have done for forty years. When it comes to the compulsion to repeat exasperating patterns, the wisdom of experience does not seem to hold much sway. Indeed, it is often when we think that we have finally broken a pattern—when we are confident that we will at long last be able to reach a better outcome—that we, once again, find ourselves in the same tiresome scenario. After a while, this repetition can make us feel helpless in relation to our own lives, so that, as Freud expressed the matter, we come to suspect that our destinies are dictated by a "daemonic" force over which we have little control.[2] It is as if our lives were not fully "ours" but rather guided by an invisible power that does not always have our best interests in mind.

When we are struggling in the tentacles of the repetition compulsion, it is easy to feel as if we were "sentenced" to a particular kind of life—as if the direction of our destiny were so firmly fixed that there is no point in trying to alter our course. We can in fact become so resigned to our lot that we lose the ability to envision alternatives to the psychological and emotional configurations that shape our daily existence; we begin to feel that no matter what we do, the result will always be the same, so that we give up the attempt to imagine something different. In this manner, we narrow the field of existential options available to us, thereby drastically limiting what is achievable in our lives. We step into a personal geography of well-defined and well-defended borders, with the consequence that our movements become restricted and highly standardized: we allow ourselves to follow certain kinds of life directions, but not others; we cultivate certain kinds of goals and ambitions but avoid others; we approach certain kinds of people but habitually shun others. Such decisions—whether consciously or unconsciously undertaken—lend a degree of consistency to our experience in the sense that at the least we know what to expect. In a paradoxical way, we prefer the security of our misery to the insecurity of the unknown. As a result, we find ever more ingenious, ever more versatile ways to deliver ourselves to the same outcome, the same incapacitating set of circumstances; our lives are utterly predictable even as we display enormous inventiveness in always reaching the same destination.

One reason for this predictability is that the unconscious patterns of living and relating that we adopt early in our lives have a timeless quality to them: while our consciousness matures and complexifies with age, our unconscious emotional scripts are mulishly resistant to change. If we find ourselves acting like five-year-olds in personally charged situations, it is because we are driven by unconscious motivations that have not evolved much since we actually *were* five. The implications of this are disturbing, for there is something genuinely alarming about the idea that what is "running" our lives is not, after all, an invisible hand of destiny, but rather the five-year-old we once were. And although many of our unconscious patterns develop later in life, some are deeply entrenched well before we are five. Moreover, although all of our formative experiences leave a trace in our unconscious, the ones that are somehow distressing wield a special influence, which is exactly why trauma is one of the main ingredients of our identity, why who we are has a great deal to do with how we have been injured. We cannot, for instance, ever fully banish the imprint of painful childhood experiences. And because no childhood is perfect—because a child's demand for love is always bigger than what can realistically be met—none of us is completely immune to this imprint. But the intensity of our pain varies considerably, so that whereas some of us had relatively agreeable childhoods, others are coping with damaging legacies that are enormously difficult to transcend.

I have already noted the influence that our parents and other caretakers have over us when we are young, and this topic is worth revisiting because it is perhaps the most dramatic expression of our foundational vulnerability. Think about it: besides rudimentary expressions, such as crying and smiling, infants cannot do anything without others; without the presence of others, they would simply just perish. And basic things, such as how their caretakers pick them up, talk to them, or respond to their discomfort, can have life-shaping power, so that some come to expect affection, others brutality, and yet others are confused by the combination of the two. Some learn to relate in ways that lead to rewarding intimacy, whereas others discover that intimacy always brings suffering. Some learn attitudes that will bring them educational and professional success, whereas others only know how to doubt themselves and resign themselves to failure. Some learn to communicate with people in ways that meet their needs, whereas others find that people repeatedly frustrate them. Some learn how the world works, whereas others find that, for the likes of them, the world never quite works. And because we do not have conscious access to such formative influences, they are the hardest to undo and reconfigure later. In this sense, the quality of our early exposure to the world dictates a great deal about how we later experience that world.

A lot, then, depends on the hand of cards we were dealt at birth. As I have observed, we cannot choose our families or circumstances, yet because we are so dependent on the outside world, these families and circumstances have a tremendous impact on our future. As children, we do not have any choice but to become psychologically and emotionally attached to the people around us no matter how badly they treat us. We turn our budding desire toward those closest to us for the simple reason that they are the only objects available to us. Needless to say, this can be a recipe for disaster, for if our desire is met with abuse, we may spend the rest of our lives trying to pick up the pieces. Likewise, if we internalize an image of ourselves as fundamentally undeserving—if we feel resented for the very fact of taking up space in the world—it can be difficult for us to develop a viable vision of what the good life might look like for us; if we come to believe that we will always disappoint ourselves or the expectations of others, it can be hard to keep making an effort. There are, in short, countless ways for past traumas to debilitate us in the present, for the unprocessed energies of these traumas solidify into symptomatic fixations that consistently distort our relationship to the world. Even though we may rationally know that the present is nothing like the past, there are situations where that distinction is hard to maintain, where that past seems to devour the present, dictating how things are going to go.

2

Implicit in all of this is the idea that our formative experiences teach us how to desire. When we first enter the world, we do not have any psychological or emotional depth to speak of, and the bodily impulses that animate our being are undifferentiated, aimed at nothing in particular in the sense that they are aimed at everything at once.[3] However, over time, and largely as a result of our interactions with our surroundings, these impulses get channeled into specific pathways, becoming more and more organized, and taking the form of something that might be called "desire." This is how we develop the rudiments of inner life. We learn to appreciate certain things: a favorite food, our mother's touch, a comforting toy, our brother's singing, and so on. Add to this what I outlined in the previous chapter—namely, that we all experience the loss of the Thing—the loss of our primordial sense of wholeness and ontological belonging—in vastly different ways, and it becomes clear why human desire cannot be equated with a purely biological instinct to be satisfied (let alone to reproduce). Indeed, one reason I have underscored the highly specific nature of our desire is that I would like to counter our culture's tendency to collapse the distinction between the reproductive *instinct*, which many (but certainly not all) humans share with animals, on the one hand, and the socially conditioned *desire* of humans on the other.

By this distinction, I do not mean to say that humans are not animals, but merely that we are a very particular kind of animal. We are animals who have constructed an incredibly complex cultural edifice—one that consists of art, music, science, politics, economics, educational systems, bookstores, nightclubs, websites, and television shows (among other things). This edifice has an enormous influence on how we live our lives, including how we desire. Even in those cases where our desire happens to coincide with the reproductive impulse, it retains its specificity, so that we are usually not willing to sleep with just anyone to attain our objective. And more often than not, our desire has little to do with reproduction, which is why people like to have sex even when they do not want children and why they desire many other things besides sex. In part, this is due to the fact that, as I have explained, we are looking for objects (or activities) that have the power to resurrect the echo of the Thing for us. But in part it is because by the time our biological impulses attain a semiconsistent psychological and emotional valence, they have received the indelible stamp of sociality. This social element accumulates momentum incrementally, so that by the time we enter adulthood, we have acquired a relatively coherent structure of desire: we consistently want certain kinds of people, certain kinds of relational scenarios, certain kinds of goals and ambitions, as well as certain kinds of experiences and satisfactions. Even when it comes to something as basic as food, our desire is rarely merely a matter of appeasing our hunger, but of enjoying particular kinds of foods.

Our desires obviously evolve during our lifetimes. We may come to like things we used to hate or feel indifferent toward: spinach, oysters, roller-coaster rides, thick English novels, tall men with slender fingers, or short women with blond hair, for instance. And sometimes we rebel against our conditioning, opting for sexual or existential choices that go against the grain of our socialization. As I have explained, this is often necessary for feeling authentic. But even in instances where we do our very best to stay faithful to the Thing's echo, the patterns of desire we internalized as children can be hard to dissolve. And it can be equally difficult to dissolve the deposits of affect that have solidified around the sensory memory of those who once took care of us, so that we may find ourselves responding to specific relational scenarios for the simple reason that they recall earlier instances of stimulation. Unquestionably, we tend to be aroused by interpersonal dynamics that in one way or another resuscitate our formative experiences, if for no other reason than that they allow us to fantasize about the possibility of finally solving a mystery that has always haunted us. If we could never before understand why our father rejected us, perhaps we can figure it out by dating a man who does the same? If we could not understand why our mother recoiled from intense emotions, perhaps we can get to the bottom of the matter by marrying a woman who does the same? In cases such as these, our repetition compulsion is fanned by the sheer impossibility of the task. In a way, the more obstacles there are to the smooth unfolding of our desire, the more the compulsion thrives, for nothing feeds it more than the elusiveness of its goal. From this perspective, it is more or less unavoidable that we to some extent keep reliving the most traumatizing aspects of our personal history.

3

In outlining the Thing's ethical code, I stressed that the enigmatic specificity of our desire can guide us to the kinds of choices that protect our character against the banalities of conventional sociality. The repetition compulsion, in contrast, has a less felicitous outcome. Although it also articulates something about the specificity of our desire, it has frozen into a fixed attitude that strives to bar the unexpected, that strives to eliminate precisely the sort of turmoil that the Thing's startling echo tends to introduce into our lives. In other words, if our loyalty to the Thing asks us to remain receptive to what breaks the predictable surface of our daily existence, the repetition compulsion defends this surface. As a consequence, the more intractable our compulsion, the more likely it is that we will end up rejecting the very objects (or activities) that most alluringly resurrect the Thing's aura for us and that therefore hold the greatest potential for transforming our lives. Because such objects touch the primordial foundation of our being, because they usher us to the vicinity of what is most vulnerable, most undefended, within us, they may seem too risky. The repetition compulsion counters this risk by keeping us at a safe distance from such objects. The problem, of course, is that by so doing it blocks our access to objects for which we feel an unusually strong affinity; it deprives us of the possibility of the kind of incandescent satisfaction that only the Thing's echo is capable of giving us.

The distinction between the Thing's echo and the repetition compulsion may be hard to discern because both appear to communicate something about the stubbornness of our desire. The difference, however, is that while the Thing's echo connects us to what is least social about our being—and what can therefore be argued to offer a degree of resistance to cultural norms—the repetition compulsion reiterates the formative traumas of our socialization. This is exactly why the compulsion makes it hard for us to imagine lives different from the ones we are living: not only do we anticipate certain outcomes, but we end up acting in ways that guarantee that these outcomes are in fact what we receive. As a result, we start to feel powerless to change our fate even though we sense that, in some indirect way, we are its authors.[4] I do not mean to deny that there are external forces that curtail our options. We have learned that the world can be acutely forbidding not only on the level of interpersonal exchanges, but also on the level of collective injustices and inequalities. Some forms of suffering are socially generated, so that breaking a repetition compulsion will hardly solve the larger problem. I am thus not proposing that it is possible to talk about a given individual's "fate" independently of social considerations. Yet it is useful to recognize that the habitual pathways of our desire also influence how our lives turn out. Even those who manage to shatter their repetition compulsion, who manage to move in directions other than those dictated by their past, usually cannot claim an unqualified victory. Most of us slide backward from time to time, so that our best course of action might be to accept our lapses as an inevitable feature of human life.

My aim in emphasizing this tendency is not to imply that we all are doomed—that we have no say over our destinies. And it is also not to depress those with wounding personal histories. I know that the outlook I have delineated can, at first glance, be hard on those who started out with an injurious set of circumstances. But I also believe that becoming aware of the power of the repetition compulsion ultimately gives us much better tools for living a rewarding life than our attempts to minimize this power. In chapter 6, I illustrate that our greater attentiveness to the persistence of our unconscious demons can rescue us from the kinds of ethical failures that result from our tendency to underestimate this persistence. In the present context, I would like to focus on how such attentiveness allows us to use our energies more productively than we would be able to if we deluded ourselves into thinking that we can somehow just "decide" not to let the past get to us. To state the matter somewhat starkly, trusting that we can neutralize the pain of the past by choosing to ignore it does not mean that the repetition compulsion actually disappears. It merely means that we become even more stupid in relation to it—that we voluntarily throw out one of our most effective weapons against it: our consciousness of how it works.

It would be a mistake to assume that we can deactivate the repetition compulsion by ignoring, rationalizing, or overriding it. But we can learn to intervene in its insistent arc in ways that grant us a measure of agency. When we acknowledge its power, we can begin to allocate our resources to making sure that it does not run our lives without our permission. The first step in this direction is recognizing that the repetition is actually trying to help us. In a twisted sense, if the repetition keeps steering us to the same outcome, it is in part because it is striving to release a passion that has been thwarted by pain; it is striving to disperse the demons that have gathered around a traumatic experience like hungry hikers around a campfire. In its roundabout way, it is endeavoring to figure out how to bring about a more constructive result than the one we are used to getting. Essentially, its "logic" dictates that if we repeat a hurtful scenario often enough, we will eventually get it "right" (so that we will no longer be upset or disappointed). And, as convoluted as this logic may seem, it is not even entirely illogical, given that in most aspects of life it is absolutely true that practice makes perfect. It is a proven fact that the more I practice playing tennis, cooking eggplant, speaking Japanese, writing a book, preparing a legal brief, performing surgery, or lecturing to a large audience, the better I become at these activities. It is therefore not entirely senseless for me to keep repeating excruciating experiences in the hope that one day I will become so skilled at mastering them that I will defuse their power to harm me.

4

Unfortunately, when it comes to the repetition compulsion, the more we practice, the more difficult it becomes for us to see alternative possibilities; our patterns become so thoroughly entrenched that we cannot find our way out of the labyrinth of painful personal scenarios. That is, if denial is not a good solution, neither is letting the repetition continue without any arbitration. Our only real countermeasure is to develop a more active attitude toward the compulsion so that we come to recognize the moments when it is about to derail us.[5] The compulsion is at its most commanding when we remain passive pawns in its complicated game, when our responses to it are largely automatic, and particularly when we do not even realize that we are caught in its meshes. But it loses much of its momentum when we learn to block its thrust. Simply put, becoming aware of the repetition allows us to hit the pause button whenever we sense ourselves teetering at the edge of the precipice. It empowers us to ask ourselves if we really want to enter into that tired argument one more time, undertake that futile action one more time, or let ourselves be seduced by that kind of person one more time. It enables us to take a degree of distance from our psychological and emotional reactions so that we can begin to adjust our itinerary. This is what Freud had in mind when he talked about the process of making the unconscious conscious, for he understood that whatever remains unconscious is impossible to change, whereas what becomes conscious also becomes amenable to transformation.

This is how new fates become available to us. When we recognize that we do not need to allow ourselves to be drawn into a particular scenario but possess the capacity to look for other options, other paths that will take us to higher ground, we can begin to rewrite our destinies. When we sever our attachment to familiar outcomes, we develop a more agile repertoire of existential possibilities; we gain a greater measure of flexibility so that it becomes easier for us to cope with life's inevitable challenges. Equally important, when energies that have been trapped in the repetition compulsion get released, we have a huge amount of new energy available to us. This extra energy can initially feel destabilizing, but it is also exhilarating in the sense that we now have the necessary resources for activities that we might have formerly been unable to carry out. One can liken this experience to an author's breaking a writer's block: all of a sudden there is a deluge of energy that can be used productively rather than symptomatically; there is the possibility of growth in all kinds of directions that might have been previously unimaginable.[6] If a passive relationship to our repetition compulsion signifies an inner deadness of sorts—a state of being helplessly wedged in our unconscious conflicts—breaking the repetition revitalizes us, ushering us into the midst of a new kind of life. Some of us may be able to achieve this break on our own. But many of us need professional help: we often need someone else's wits to learn how to outwit our most fate-defining patterns so that different patterns become conceivable to us.

I have implied that there is a wisdom in loving our fate. But this should not keep us from seeking alternative fates. If there is a contradiction here, it is only apparent, for it is possible to love our fate while also striving to refashion it. On the one hand, to the degree that we cannot escape our fate—that it is ours to live through—we have no choice but to own it; we have no choice but to take responsibility for it in the sense that even when we are not the direct cause of everything that happens to us, we are to some extent the architects of our existential landscape. On the other hand, we can endeavor to rescue our character from the traumatic grip of the repetition compulsion so that the fixations of our desire gradually yield to new kinds of desires, including ones that carry a more clearly audible echo of the Thing. This process can be a bit terrifying, for there is a good chance that we will never manage to live up to the promise of our new desires. We might fail miserably, in which case we will need to reconcile ourselves to the fact of having betrayed the truth of our desire. This is why there is rarely a sense of potentiality without a degree of anxiety—why we often pay for our newly found freedom with the thumping of our hearts. Yet this thumping is also an indication that although the past exercises a great deal of influence over the present, the present does not need to replicate it entirely faithfully.

5

In the first section of this book, I spent some time talking about the ongoing process of crafting an identity. We have seen that one of the things that distinguishes humans from other animals is precisely that we are capable of this type of self-fashioning. In the same way that our imagination enables us to reinvent the world one piece at a time, it allows us to reinvent ourselves on a recurring basis; we can treat our life as a work of art in the same way that we can treat (usually modest) slices of the world as a canvas for our creative efforts. No doubt, we are always compelled to operate within the set of constraints to which we are inserted at birth and which continue to restrict our movements throughout our lives. And, no doubt, some people are better at hitting their stride among such constraints than others. But in principle all of us possess this aptitude in that it is our birthright as human beings to be capable of innovation. What I have done in this chapter is to add another layer to this line of reasoning by showing that being able to intervene in our unconscious patterns is an essential part of our art of living. Without it, our attempts at self-constitution remain superficial at best, unable to reach the fundamentals of our character.

When we allow ourselves to be driven by our unconscious fixations, our relationship to our lives remains largely reactive and therefore far from artistic. A more active stance, in contrast, enables us to see that unconscious patterns are an important part of our process of becoming a particular kind of person and that it is consequently only by breaking such patterns that we can become a different kind of person. One might even say that how we grapple with the unique challenges posed by the repetition compulsion is one of the most character-refining components of our lives. As long as our art of living incorporates only what is conscious, it merely peruses the periphery of our lives so that our understanding of ourselves as well as our ability to steer ourselves to the desired outcome are limited. But when we manage to negotiate our way out of our unconscious fixations, we bring about a drastic reorientation of passion. This is one way to understand what self-responsibility might entail in the context of lives that recognize the centrality of the unconscious to the human predicament.[7]

Let me restate the matter as follows: when we realize that we do not need to reconcile ourselves to the version of our lives that we have inherited from our past, we can begin to detach ourselves from its more distressing elements. Although there are people who are perfectly happy with the familial and social legacies that have formed them, many of us can take some comfort in the knowledge that we are not condemned to live forever in the fold of these legacies. And it may be particularly important for those with difficult personal histories to comprehend that they are not prisoners of their past—that even though they cannot undo the past, they can to some extent change the ways in which it operates in the present. Even if, as I have conceded, it might be impossible for us to ever wholly reverse the psychological and emotional effects of the past, we are never merely its helpless victims. We can, among other things, work at expunging internalized sediments of self-hatred in order to convert an abject image of ourselves into something more life affirming. Or—to return to a point I made in the context of Nietzsche—we can work at reinterpreting an agonizing experience from the past as a constructive influence on our character, so that if we, say, possess a heightened capacity for empathy, we come to see that this is not in spite of but *because* of this experience.

6

Throughout my discussion, I have stressed that the fact that we feel primordially lacking—that we rarely feel completely whole and self-realized—is what causes us to reach for objects and activities beyond ourselves. What I am saying now is related in the sense that our awareness of being wounded by the past can become a catalyst for our continuous efforts to bring more evolved versions of ourselves into being. These efforts can become obsessive, as when we spend hours at the gym pursuing the perfect body, when we exhaust ourselves by working overly long hours, when we berate ourselves for relationship failures that are not our fault, or when we become so charitable and other oriented that we forget to take care of ourselves. When it comes to painting our personal masterpiece, we can definitely take things too far; we can become so invested in our goals and ambitions that we never give ourselves a break. Even our quest for the notoriously elusive peace of mind can cross the line to pathology, so that we spend huge amounts of energy on spiritual practices that are supposed to guide us to our destination, but that actually keep us from living our lives. But none of this changes the fact that the pain of the past can spur us to various forms of self-reflexivity and self-development.

This is precisely why I have placed so much emphasis on the notion that even the most intolerable components of the past can become valuable constituents of the present. It is why I have argued that there is a deep connection between the ways in which we have been traumatized and the ever-evolving singularity of our being—that crafting a character is, in part at least, a matter of transmuting the raw materials supplied by the past into a present reality that to some (always limited) extent corresponds to our ideals. I do not mean that every torturous detail of our past is worth resurrecting; there is no need either to glorify or fetishize pain or to assume that every morsel of it must be turned into meaning. In the same way that there are times when a loss is a pure loss—when nothing good comes out of a loss—there are times when pain is just pain, when it does not lead to anything productive. And there are also times when we get hurt so badly that we cannot find our way out of our pit of despair, let alone transform this despair into something useful. Yet it is also clear that there are few things in life that serve our art of living more than our ability to distill pain into some sort of existential insight.

Suffering washes away what is superfluous; it dissolves impurities so that we can access a more gracious version of ourselves. This is why people who have undergone difficult ordeals are frequently more interesting, more multifaceted, than those who have not. To the extent that they have harnessed the wisdom stored up in their pain, they possess an intensity of character that is palpable to anyone who comes in contact with them. Those who understand this also understand Nietzsche's claim that all of our past experiences, including the most devastating, have contributed to our formation, so that unless we would prefer to be someone else, we need to accept these experiences as a part of who we are. In this chapter, I have tried to deepen our understanding of why this acceptance is not the same thing as letting the legacies of pain control our destinies. Nietzsche himself underscored this point, albeit in a somewhat problematic manner: he thought that noble characters should be able to simply shrug off their hurtful histories in order to create space for stronger versions of themselves. I have less faith in our capacity to do so, not the least because I have more respect for the often quite inscrutable densities of unconscious life. But I share his belief that being able to make good use of the past within the framework of our current conditions is a sign of existential acumen; I share his view that because life without suffering is unrealistic, the best we can do with the pain of the past is to turn it into a resource for living in the present.

7

I call attention to this view in part to counteract our society's pervasive conviction that those who have been damaged by the past are irrevocably broken or at least severely disfigured. On the one hand, the American dream dictates that there is no limit to what we can achieve. On the other, our therapeutic culture implies those who have suffered a great deal are unable to catch the current of life with the same nimbleness as those who have been more fortunate. It is, for instance, common to think that those who grew up in dysfunctional families find it unusually difficult to build supportive relationships. Undoubtedly, this is sometimes the case because, as we have learned, the repetition compulsion wields a great deal of influence. I myself have admitted—and will continue to do so— that it can be harder for those who have been traumatized to see the world as a space of possibility. But I also know that it is easy to overstate the issue; it is easy to form misleading (and patronizing) judgments about those who have led pain-filled lives. After all, it may well be that those struggling with a history of hardship have learned to live and relate more effectively than those who have not gone through the same demanding apprenticeship.

There is no need to presume that those who have suffered have been weakened by their trials. Quite the contrary, it may be that they have gained an added layer of ingenuity from these trials. Even though hardship can certainly accumulate over time so that sometimes it takes very little to send us over the edge, it can also make us tougher so that the more of it we have experienced, the more skilled we are at coping with new instances of it. Unquestionably, when the trauma of the present coincides too closely with the trauma of the past, it can be difficult to avoid a breakdown. And the less we are able to articulate the sources of our suffering, the more volatile this suffering becomes. But, in principle, there is no reason to assume that those who have been traumatized invariably have lower thresholds—that they cannot bear more damage without collapsing. I suspect that the opposite is frequently the case so that those who have survived hardship know how to survive it again. As a result, they are not rattled by the first sign of it but are able to face it more courageously. Over the years, they have developed enough psychological and emotional limberness to jump over hurdles with a degree of poise and sometimes even a dash of elegance.

Out of the ability to outlive hardship arises the kind of personal power that makes us more able to cope with life's myriad adversities. The capacity to metabolize—not just to endure, but to metabolize—suffering is an indication of the kind of robustness of spirit that does not allow suffering to become an immovable component of our being (unless, of course, we are subject to the kind of physical suffering that cannot be banished). It is a sign that we are unwilling to let suffering take up permanent residency within our interiority. This is not a matter of pretending that this suffering is not real. Rather, it is a matter of gradually rendering it malleable so that it can be translated into something else. This "something else" may be nothing more than a more muted form of suffering; sometimes the best we can do is to take the sting out of our suffering. But this is already a huge achievement, for it confirms that we are versatile enough to convert our suffering into discomfort, nostalgia, and other lesser forms of evil. In this way, we make our pain more livable. And sometimes we even turn its residue into an essential component of the new fate that we are in the process of actualizing.

I have suggested that when self-fashioning becomes an obsession, we engage in a corruption of life rather than its augmentation. Pursuing new editions of ourselves is not the same thing as pursuing perfection, wholeness, or a complete lack of pain. It is not a matter of accomplishing the impossible, but rather of attaining higher levels of complexity, suppleness, discernment, and interpersonal penetration; it is a matter of seeing the glass as half full rather than half empty, so that we are able to recognize when life is satisfying enough—when it is as satisfying as it can get within certain limitations. The goal of this chapter has been to demonstrate that the more we accept responsibility for our unconscious blueprints of behavior, the better our chances of building a life that feels worth living. And it has also been to reconsider the role of affliction in our lives, so that we no longer define the good life as a life devoid of pain, but rather as one where pain gets metamorphosed, however incompletely, into resourcefulness. From this point of view, one might even speculate that a person who has not known sadness is not a fully realized person. She has not been properly tested in the sense that her resilience has not been adequately assessed. Nor has she had the opportunity to determine where her limits lie, where the distinction between what is bearable to her and what is not resides. This is why pain, even repetitive pain, is not necessarily the antithesis of character, but rather one of its reinforcements.

5

The Alchemy of Relationality

For the confirmation of my identity I depend entirely upon other people.

—Hannah Arendt

1

I have emphasized that human beings are by definition precariously open to the world—that who we become depends in large part on how we interact with our surroundings. And, arguably, there is nothing about the external world that has a bigger impact on us than other people. To assert that there is no self without others, as I have implicitly done, is to acknowledge that our lives are made up of a complex tissue of alterity. Because we are born into a preexisting network of sociality, and particularly because of the infantile vulnerability I have highlighted, there is no way even to begin to think about our lives independently of others. And what makes our predicament doubly demanding is that we are not only dealing with the conscious thoughts and life choices of those we interact with, but also with their unconscious blueprints of behavior, including their unprocessed (or half-processed) repetition compulsions. We are inserted into webs of relationality where invisible currents of energy crisscross in highly unpredictable ways. In this sense, it is not only the case, as Hannah Arendt states, that we depend upon others for the confirmation of our identity—which is certainly true.[1] It is also that we often have no way of knowing ahead of time how this dependence is going to play itself out; we have no way of anticipating where our relationships will take us.

Because other people are partially inscrutable in the sense that we cannot always know what they are thinking, how they are feeling, or what their intentions are, we are frequently to some extent mystified by them. Even when we ask them to account for themselves, we may not get an accurate answer because, like us, they are guided by unconscious passions that they may not fully understand. This is not to say that all of human behavior is incomprehensible. Because we share a common sociocultural environment—one that gives us a collective set of tools for approaching others—we can often understand each other relatively well, provided we are willing to make an effort; we can make educated guesses about the inner states of others based on our own reactions as well as on our life experience. But a portion of what goes on between people—the unconscious portion of relationality—is always a little ambiguous.

Again, this starts in childhood. When we are young, we often cannot figure out what our parents or other adults want from us. Their communications, and particularly their unspoken desires, remain shrouded in mystery. As Jean Laplanche, among others, has noted, we spend much of our formative years responding to the enigmatic desires that surround us, and over time we can start to feel overwhelmed by our repeated failure to understand these desires.[2] Particularly when this failure is coupled with the fear of punishment, our uncertainty can become so acute that we fall into a habitual state of overagitation. Although it is not common to think of anxiety as a childhood phenomenon, many children cope with high levels of daily tension that result from their incessant efforts to decode (and thereby neutralize) disorienting or otherwise distressing messages aimed at them. And it does not matter whether this stress is rationally warranted or not, whether the perceived threat is real or not, for even compassionate adults can confuse a child merely by virtue of the fact that there is an unbridgeable gap between the cognitive resources of adulthood and childhood. Adults can, in short, induce terror in children without realizing that this is what they are doing; their desires may seem formidable even when there is no conscious intent to intimidate. Consequently, when children recoil from the adult world, it is frequently because they are faced by enigmatic bundles of desire they cannot quite make sense of.

Many of us are thoroughly stressed out, not only psychologically and emotionally, but even physically, well before we reach adulthood. And, obviously, such deep-seated buildups of anxiety are difficult to banish later, so that some of us end up living our entire lives in the same state of mental and bodily overalertness as we experienced as children. Despite the fact that our lives may now be completely different and that we may now have much more control over our environment, we cannot necessarily drive out the layers of excess tension that have taken hold of our being; even when there is no nameable basis for anxiety, we cannot always relax our overvigilant attitude in relation to the world because, on a visceral level, we cannot convince ourselves that this world is truly benign. And if this is to some degree the case even with those who grew up in supportive environments—environments where adults were not abusive but merely a little cryptic—it is clearly much more drastically true of those who endured a great deal of maltreatment. As I have acknowledged, one of the most insidious aspects of abusive childhoods is that their effects persist indefinitely, so that when a new traumatic event, however obliquely, touches the imprint of earlier trauma, it can be hard to keep ourselves from unraveling. In such instances, we are plunged back into an all too familiar landscape of anxiety that causes us to overreact to the situation at hand even when the more rational part of us is telling us to calm down.

2

Our tendency to get agitated by interpersonal enigmas does not end at the onset of adulthood, for even those who for the most part escaped it as children may not be entirely immune to it later in life. Think of what happens when a lover (or a potential lover) becomes difficult to read. Suddenly we want nothing more than to be able to crack his or her code, and our failure to do so can drive us to distraction. There may even be times when our attraction to a person results primarily from our inability to decipher his or her motivations, so that the moment this person becomes more transparent, our interest wanes. The overagitation of romantic love—its proverbial flutter of butterflies—is frequently more or less identical to the overagitation of not being able to penetrate the mystery that the beloved represents. This is obviously quite different from the overagitation caused by childhood terror in the sense that we tend to actively pursue it: we often *want* to feel unsettled by love. But even here, the line between pleasure and pain can get fuzzy, particularly with respect to people who exploit this dynamic, purposely cultivating an aura of inscrutability so as to gain control over others. Indeed, straight women in our culture are explicitly trained to do so by being told to "play hard to get" (among other relationship games).[3] Yet there is an immense difference between the temporary arousal of passion generated by unavailability and a genuinely reciprocal relationship; there is a difference between being able to awaken someone's curiosity and being able to build an alliance that meets the needs of both partners.

Equally often, others overstimulate us without meaning to, as is the case when our bosses, mentors, or colleagues neglect to clarify some detail that seems obscurely important to us or when our doctor leaves us a vague message about needing to schedule a test of some kind. And sometimes our anxiety rises for entirely trivial reasons, say, when we cannot figure out why the bank teller is taking so long with the person in front of us or why the waiter in a crowded restaurant serves later arrivals before serving us. Even completely impersonal structures, such as government bureaucracies, immigration authorities, and insurance agencies, can cause our stress level to climb whenever they make demands that seem irrelevant. When they ask for this or that form, for proof of this or that activity, we can exhaust ourselves by our futile efforts to work out the rationale of it all. Whenever we are asked to account for ourselves in ways that we cannot comprehend, and particularly when the authorities in question appear to act on a whim so that we are left wondering about their intentions, chances are there are psychological, emotional, and sometimes even physiological consequences.

In this context, it is important to be aware of the uneven force of such impersonal mysteries. Those who lead intensely insecure lives—who feel that their existence is a constant battle for survival—are particularly vulnerable to such mysteries. If you are poor, black, and female, being stopped by a police officer for no apparent reason has a greater impact than if you are rich, white, and male. Although much depends on the personal history of the individual, economic status, skin color, and gender (among other identity markers) can make a huge difference in determining how terrifying (or frustrating) a given situation is. Likewise, something as simple as crossing a national border can have vastly different effects depending on one's relationship to the authority figures who monitor who gets in and who does not. If you carry a European passport, crossing the border between France and Germany is a no-brainer. But if you carry a Pakistani or Chinese passport, it can be petrifying. And crossing the U.S. border is almost invariably more stress inducing than crossing the border to Switzerland, even for many American citizens. This is in part because U.S. immigration laws give officers the right to bar entry, and sometimes even detain people, without offering them any kind of an explanation. This uncertainty can cause anxiety even in people who in principle have nothing to worry about.

My overall point is that how we are situated in relation to both impersonal and interpersonal networks of power has a massive impact on how safe we feel. Those who feel socially disempowered as well as those who feel at a disadvantage in a vital personal or professional relationship are much more susceptible to excess agitation (and its psychological, emotional, and physiological consequences) than those who wield more authority. And sometimes there is even a degree of crossover between the impersonal and interpersonal levels, so that an individual who lives under constant social anxiety may also feel a higher level of anxiety in his or her personal or professional relationships. As a result, the next time we are tempted to tell our partner that he or she is asking too many questions or acting pathetically insecure, we might want to consider the larger structures of uncertainty that surround him or her. There may well be a link between our partner's behavior and his or her relationship to more impersonal systems of power. Some people have very good reasons for being socially paranoid, so that we cannot exactly blame them for being a little paranoid in more intimate settings as well. And none of us is entirely immune to such paranoia, so that we often end up wasting a great deal of energy in trying to solve the various conundrums that besiege us. Even when we know that our efforts are largely pointless, we cannot necessarily help ourselves; we cannot keep the outside world out of our minds no matter how hard we try. This is how we come to lie awake at night, tossing and turning, spinning mental spirals as convoluted as one of Hitchcock's celebrated staircases. In such cases, our psyches cannot rest because they have been pushed into too high a gear by the mysterious messages around us.

3

Yet, as is the case with so much of human life, there is a flipside to all of this—namely, that if our ontological openness to others makes our lives more precarious, it also brings tremendous advantages. I have already observed that the reverse of our vulnerability in relation to the world is that we are also the beneficiaries of its more benevolent influences. Likewise, if other people—consciously or unconsciously—rouse our anxieties, they can also help us fulfill more of our potential by inducing us to access facets of ourselves that we might not be able to access on our own. When others treat us well, and sometimes even when they do not, they often manage to activate dimensions of our interiority that would otherwise dissolve into silence; by giving prominence to this or that attribute, this or that predilection, they may animate frequencies of our being that remain dormant, repressed, or difficult to arouse. For instance, a friend's persistent encouragement may allow us to arrive at a more charitable reading of ourselves than we are accustomed to. A mentor can push us to higher levels of achievement by applying just the right amount of pressure. And a lover's soothing caress may allow us to drop the guarded demeanor demanded by the exertions of public life, so that we can relax into our minds and bodies, reclaiming modalities of being that might have gotten lost in the general commotion of living.

The more intimate our relationships, the more potential they hold for allowing us to make contact with disclaimed aspects of ourselves. One reason we covet romantic alliances is that they tend to function as keys that unlock the secret chambers of our interiority, resuscitating facets of our character that have been subdued or otherwise marginalized. Love, as it were, extends a generous summons to the clandestine sediments of personality we have learned to conceal from the world.[4] The implications of this are enormous, for there is something uniquely vitalizing about giving buried components of our being the permission to rise to the surface. What has been silenced suddenly gets to speak; what has been neglected leaps out into the open; what has been abandoned is readmitted into the fray of life. Although this experience can be a little disquieting, it is usually also deeply inspiring, for there are few things in life that feel better than being able to release bottled-up affects without the fear of rejection. When this happens, we may feel that we have finally stumbled upon a life that genuinely feels worth living. In this sense, love is not only a matter of two people coming together in a passionate manner, but also a means for both partners to explore new levels of self-experience and relational capacity; it is a means for both to approach their process of self-fashioning from a previously foreclosed perspective.

Intimate relationships, at their best, can help us break out of false self-presentations, so that we get to experience a freer, less rigid version of ourselves. False self-presentations are usually designed to protect us from injury. They facilitate our survival, yet they also impoverish us by making it impossible for the world's enabling influences to reach us. Those we relate to intimately—lovers and close friends—may have a way of getting around our defenses. Although we may be able to fool our surroundings in less personal settings, those closest to us generally sense when something is amiss, unless they themselves are so snugly lodged in their own fortress that they cannot risk venturing out. Undeniably, as I argue later, there are intimate relationships that fail to activate anything authentic about the individuals involved—that remain superficial because both parties studiously avoid stirring the deeper waters of relationality for fear of muddying them. But frequently intimate relationships have the power to coax us out of our armor, even if they do so only tentatively and for fleeting stretches of time.

4

Given that this is the case—that our relationships generate the kind of transformative energy that can be literally life shaping—what most astonishes me is how many of us approach our closest alliances in a thoroughly absentminded manner. Furthermore, what is perhaps most noteworthy about contemporary forms of interpersonality is how obstinately we tend to hold on to alliances that are either utterly uninteresting or deeply tiresome. In part, this is because we live in a society that engages in a purely habitual valorization of relationality, so that we are programmed to believe that having a relationship is invariably better than not having one, no matter how mediocre, how trite and hackneyed, this relationship may be. We are, for instance, conditioned to assume that those without intimate partners or extensive social networks are somehow defective or at the very least tremendously unlucky;

we are conditioned to think that they are lonely and miserable, secretly (and desperately) yearning to assemble the kinds of relational constellations that others fall into effortlessly. All of this can lead us to forget what I stressed in chapter 2—namely, that living a meaningful life entails the capacity to discriminate between relationships that are inspiring and others that are not; it can lead us to forget that insipid relationships, far from allowing us to actualize our character, may actually make it harder for us to hear its call.

Take our society's insistence on marriage as the pinnacle of human existence. Even a cursory survey of our songs, movies, magazines, commercials, self-help guides, and other shapers of romantic culture reveals that our society consistently portrays singleness as a state of wretchedness that needs to be overcome as quickly as possible.[5] According to such portrayals, there is nothing as important as being able to erase singleness by the delights of romance, coupledom, and family life. Singleness is, as it were, an anomaly, a temporary state of being that is expected to be abandoned as soon as someone appropriate comes along. As a matter of fact, there is almost no cultural space for imagining scenarios where we would opt for singleness even when the "right" partner is available. The assumption is that if we are single, it is because we have not yet managed to find "the One." Or perhaps it is because we are incapable of successful relating owing to some prior romantic disappointment? Prolonged singlehood, from this perspective, is a sign of malfunction and sometimes even of existential failure; it carries the stigma of emptiness, desolation, depression, and despair, so that being alone becomes one of the worst things that could ever happen to us.

This way of looking at things obscures the fact that there can be a great deal of emptiness, desolation, depression, and despair within committed relationships, that the day-to-day reality of long-term alliances frequently has little to do with the idyllic representations that dominate our culture. I am of course not saying that all marriages are soul slaying—far from it. Yet it is true that many people are desperately lonely within their marriages. Countless others feel misunderstood or otherwise neglected. And many alliances are essentially "dead" in the sense that they are held together by routine, convenience, obligation, or fear of loneliness rather than by any real connection between the partners.

The feeling of depletion that can overtake us in such alliances is not wholly unlike the enervation that can steal upon us when we are overexposed to shallow forms of sociality in our public lives, as when we, for example, have to sit in crowded subway cars, work in crowded settings, or walk on crowded sidewalks. One of Arendt's many contributions to our intellectual heritage is to have analyzed such a compression of space in modern society. In her view, contemporary urban life, communications technology, and the relative ease of travel have shrunk the distance between people to such an extent that we sometimes feel as if we were constantly (and unwillingly) rubbing elbows with strangers.[6] That is, though Arendt acknowledges our foundational dependence on others, she also warns us against the more anesthetizing aspects of sociality. When others are too close, too insistently in our space—when the crowd is encroaching from every direction—it is difficult to hold on to a sense of individual identity. In such circumstances, being with others hardly alleviates our loneliness but merely aggravates it. In a way, crowded spaces force us to live on the surface because the surface is the only thing that the crowd understands.

What many of us habitually overlook is that intimate relationships that have lost their momentum can have a very similar impact. Indeed, we are often willing to work at such relationships to an almost irrational degree; we would rather invest our time, effort, and emotions in relationships that bring us no reward than concede that long-term relationships are not always necessarily the haven of harmony we are taught to envision. It is as if there were a cultural conspiracy calculated to conceal all the ways in which the institution of marriage can be damaging and draining, not to mention outright abusive. I obviously do not think that this "conspiracy" is intentional; I know that there is no secret society of opinion makers sitting in some backroom plotting the downfall of single people, though the Christian Right may sometimes come close (particularly with respect to the much maligned category of single mothers). Yet there is no doubt that things have evolved in such a way that it is very difficult for us to see that there are situations where being alone is infinitely more enlivening than being trapped in an alliance that suffocates us. And it is equally difficult to admit that bad relationships can constrict our universe by depriving us of promising life directions; it is surprisingly difficult to admit that they can channel our (always limited) resources into personal choices that do not actually reflect the truth of our desire.

5

Many of us use relationships to organize our existence. In principle, there is nothing wrong with doing this. But I think that it is useful to recognize that it is a thoroughly ideological choice—one that we make often for no other reason than that we have been taught to think that the payoffs of relationality are intrinsically higher than being alone. Yet a moment's reflection reveals that this is not always the case. High levels of creativity, for instance, frequently require periods of solitude, for there is nothing that smothers the creative impulse more quickly than constant exposure to external stimuli. This is why Virginia Woolf famously argued that an artist—in her case, the woman writer—needs a room of her own to create, that it is virtually impossible to bring into being works of great value when one is caught up in the provocations and aggravations of everyday existence.[7] Every instant spent worrying about some practical detail of life, such as a relationship entanglement, is an instant stolen away from alternative preoccupations, including creativity. Although this is not the case for everyone, although there are those whose creativity thrives in the company of others, solitude is for many a means of keeping the world's intrusiveness at bay.

Solitary individuals are often judged as pathological or condemned as selfish. Yet, realistically, there are limits to how much any of us can accomplish. It is difficult to deny that those who are predominantly focused on relationships have fewer resources available for other kinds of activities. On this account, those opt-ing for solitude over relationships—particularly troubled ones—may well be choosing wisely. They know that there can be a cer-tain restfulness and self-sufficiency to solitary pursuits. Solitude, in other words, opens up an array of existential possibilities that are closed to those who are incapable of it. As a consequence, what may, from the outside, seem like an impoverished life may actually be uniquely rich and satisfying, for when we look beyond the con-fines of everyday sociality, we can sometimes see further; we can discern distant horizons of insight that the normative customs of relationality tend to render imperceptible. Precisely because soli-tude, however provisionally, liberates us from our social obliga-tions and interpersonal involvements, it is conducive to the emer-gence of alternative worlds of wonder. And it may even be that solitude recharges us so that we have more to give to others when we emerge from it. After all, the more self-connected we feel, the better we are at sustaining authentic relationships.

I am by no means suggesting that we all should become world-shunning hermits. I hope to have made it clear that I believe that relationality resides at the heart of human life. I am merely try-ing to show that our culture's equation of intimate relationships with healing, happiness, fulfillment, and self-completion can sometimes make it difficult for us to appreciate other things that may be equally valuable. For example, some of us spend years, even decades, obsessing over the fact that we do not have love even though our lives are filled with a multitude of alternative sources of gratification (such as thriving careers, close friendships, or strongly stimulating goals and ambitions). I can hear the objec-tions. Everyone, we are told, needs love! Everyone needs a bit of romance and someone to rely on. But is this really the case? What about all the other ways we can fashion a worthwhile life? And what about other things we seem to "need" but often don't get? Surely there are other goals and ambitions that also routinely slip through our fingers. Thinking that love is a special commodity without which our lives are meaningless gives it disproportionate power, blinding us to the possibility that it may not be any more important than many of our other (realized or unrealized) aspirations. In contrast, when we place relationality in a proper perspective, when we view it as merely one component of our process of becoming, we may be able to better appreciate our lives even when we do not have a constant supply of love.

Against this backdrop, we might want to rethink what it means to leave a relationship. Although the alchemy of good relationships can be life enhancing, this alchemy is not always possible to maintain across time; in part because people evolve at different paces, the growth of a relationship does not always coincide with the growth of those involved. As a result, when we flee a relationship that no longer feels viable, we are not necessarily narrowing our existential repertoire but, quite the opposite, expanding it. Admittedly, this possibility can be hard to assess accurately, particularly because we often find it difficult to envision the wake of a relationship as anything but a loss. But this is all the more reason to admit that sometimes the best way to achieve the aims of our spirit is to sidestep particular people, particular relationships. Indeed, whenever we feel tempted to run from a relationship, it is likely that we are running toward something else. Although this something might be another relationship, it might also be seemingly unconnected to relationships. There are even times when we have only a vague premonition of what our aspiration might be. Yet we intuit that we can attain it only by freeing ourselves from a relationship that is keeping us from pursuing it.

Our patterns of avoidance can be as essential to our overall well-being as our patterns of intimacy. Paradoxically enough, escaping can be a way of expressing desire, even if we cannot yet designate the precise object of that desire. This type of partially unreadable desire is not necessarily any less valid than our desire for what we already know; our desire for some undefinable thing in the future is in principle no less authentic than our desire for what we have in the present. Understanding this may make it easier for us to renounce worn-out relationships. And it may also help us realize that when others leave us, it is not always because we did something to alienate them or even because there was something intrinsically wrong with the relationship, but because they felt compelled to follow the enigmatic summons of an inchoate desire they could not yet quite put into words; they may not have been able to explain why they needed to get away, yet there may have been a great deal of integrity to their decision to end the relationship.

6

Undoubtedly there are relationships that are worth holding on to even when they are ailing; undoubtedly we can often burrow our way through the obstacles so that the relationship once again becomes feasible and sometimes even better than before. But a simple shift in perspective might help us assess things differently in those cases where we are striving to revive a relationship that is clearly past its expiration date. If we understood relationships as fickle entities that are not always meant to endure—if we came to accept as a "given" that people have the tendency to outgrow relationships—we might be less enthusiastic about expending energy on ones that are hurtful or otherwise floundering. Even if a given relationship was once the best thing that ever happened to us, it may no longer have anything positive to contribute. Why, then, would we want to prolong it artificially (thereby slowly destroying the memory of what was once marvelous about it)? Why would we allow ourselves to get stuck in a relationship that has lost its traction?

Although some relationships obviously flourish and endure, many do not. In effect, some of our most magnificent alliances are ones that ultimately fail. By this I do not mean to advocate callousness toward our loved ones, let alone imply that we should abandon relationships carelessly. For one thing, I believe that we have an ethical obligation to the people we have loved so that we do not have the right to discard them in whichever way we want to. There are, in short, more or less honorable ways to end a relationship. At the same time, trying to mend a broken bond usually merely postpones the inevitable. In addition, whenever we take it for granted that saving a relationship is better than breaking it, we assume that the gold standard for relationships is longevity rather than, say, the relationship's continued ability to animate us. But why should we assume this? And why should we rank our loyalty to a faltering, spirit-dampening relationship above the part of us that is hungry for a different kind of life? Looked at in this light, relationship losses are not so much failures as important vehicles for change. They force us to leave some things behind so as to create space for other things; they teach us that a certain amount of death is necessary for rebirth.

When we are lucky, our relationships change with us, so that there is no tension between them and our ability to reach new incarnations of ourselves. And there may even be times where we manage to recapture the luster of a relationship that has lost it. I have proposed that desire is a matter of discovering the sublime echo of the Thing in a mundane object. And I have pointed out that there is a great deal of flexibility to our desire not only in the sense that we can shift between objects, but also in the sense that we can appreciate one object in various ways at different points in time. This implies that good relationships often stay good in part because we are able to bring the latter kind of flexibility to bear on them, because we are able to honor the ever-evolving nature of our chosen object by inventing novel ways to desire it. As a consequence, our relationship does not turn stale, but merely different; we do not outgrow it but grow with every new incarnation it takes. In contrast, those who are incapable of such flexibility of desire—those who demand that their object stay eternally the same in order to remain desirable—will find it difficult to maintain enduring relationships. To the extent that they remain devoted to an outdated image of what the object should be, every deviation from this image becomes a source of irritation. This is one reason that it is important, as I have emphasized, to work on keeping our desire limber. Those whose desire has congealed into unyielding configurations will find it virtually impossible to let their alliances breathe. They hold on too tightly, with the result that they squeeze the life out of their relationships.

7

When we hold on too tightly, it is often because we have internalized our society's belief that relationships are meant to bring stability to our lives. Many of us in fact attribute to intimate relationships an almost magical power to rescue us from the turbulence of existence. But, regrettably, the safety they seem to provide is frequently deceptive at best, for few things in life are as erratic as intimate relationships. It is, quite simply, not in the nature of eros to be disciplined. It routinely rejects our rationalizations and outmaneuvers our best-laid plans. In addition, the more we try to manipulate it, the less we are able to experience what is truly life altering about it; our attempts to control it kill its soul, robbing it of everything that is noble about it. In a way, we expect from it what it is not meant to deliver: we expect the kind of reliability that wars against the (basically mischievous) spirit of eros.

This is not to say that our partnerships cannot offer solace against the turmoil of living. They can certainly make us feel more grounded. And they can provide comfort during difficult passages. But, ultimately, there are no guarantees. Even solemn vows cannot alter the fact that relationships have a way of falling apart, wearing out, shifting beyond recognition, and disappointing us beyond repair. It is the very essence of relationships—particularly of romantic ones—to be mutable. Love ebbs and flows in a capricious manner. We lose it. We misplace it. We refind it. We lose it again. This is why the expectation of permanence that we bring to our romantic alliances may be overly optimistic. Although the institutionalization of love through marriage may offer a promise of solidity, there is always something hollow about this promise in the sense that although it can prop up the institution (marriage), it cannot prop up the emotion (love). One might in fact speculate that when romance disenchants us, it is not necessarily because something went wrong, but because our outlook is too conventional. If we learned to ask different things from love—say, aliveness and adventure rather than permanence—we might be less frustrated by it.

Love without risk is an oxymoron. Yet our culture does its best to convince us that there is a way to dissociate love from the danger of getting hurt. Even though we are taught to love love, we are also relentlessly warned against its mirages; we are constantly told that "real" love is the opposite of the impetuous, elating experience of falling in love. Personally, I have little patience with this advice; I have little patience with the idea that love should be a wholly levelheaded enterprise divorced from all transcendent aspirations.

Take the common conviction that idealizing our lover is a mistake for which we will eventually pay with disillusionment. I do not deny that our ideals can sometimes mislead us. And, as I admitted in chapter 3, when idealization becomes a way of feeding our narcissistic quest for wholeness, it degenerates into a frighteningly self-serving enterprise that suffocates the very person we are supposed to love. But I am equally wary of the notion that love should be stripped of all ideals, for this would amount to declaring that our lover is not worthy of the veneration we choose to bestow upon him or her. Moreover, though we are conditioned to think that our assessment of our lover as ordinary is more reliable than our idealizing assessment of him or her as extraordinary, this may not in fact be the case; there is absolutely no guarantee that our appraisal of our beloved as banal is any more correct than our evaluation of him or her as sublime. After all, as I have maintained, we never have transparent access to another person's inner world. Against this backdrop, the uplifting sweep of idealization can be argued to be merely an indulgent way to interpret the intangible (and always slightly mystifying) reality of the person we love; it can be said to be a generous means of bringing into the foreground and perhaps even awakening sediments of his or her being that might otherwise remain marginalized.[8]

Our world is already so levelheaded, so relentlessly practical, that we sometimes need the energizing jolt of love to be able to see clearly. According to this account, when we idealize a person, we illuminate aspects of him or her that everyday life tends to force into hibernation; we raise to prominence a version of the beloved that only the adoring attitude of romantic love is able to conjure into existence. As a result, although idealization, taken to an extreme, can violate our lover's integrity, the opposite strategy of demoting him or her to a wholly prosaic object denies the fact that love needs some evidence of transcendence. It denies the fact that if our desire crystallizes around a particular person with unusual force, it is because this person contains a shining sliver of sublimity (a uniquely compelling manifestation of the Thing's echo) that makes him or her inestimably valuable to us, that explains why only *this* person will do and why our love for this person is nonnegotiable. In this sense, love may be one of the few things we experience that has the power to induce the sublime to materialize within the framework of daily life. That is, love is not merely—as many of us are inclined to believe—what deludes us into thinking that we can access the sublime, but what, in a very real (tangible) manner, does actually make the sublime available to us.[9] In the last chapter of this book, I talk about other ways of capturing the sublime within the folds of everyday reality. For now, let me simply note that when it comes to honoring the call of our character, it may be that nothing is quite as important as protecting the sublime aura of what we love against the pragmatic thrust of our society, for this aura connects us to something that not only feels inimitable, but in many ways actually *is* inimitable.

At first glance, it may seem that there is a conflict between my wish to hold on to the sublime dimensions of love and my earlier critique of the overvaluation of relationality that characterizes our society. But these views are merely two sides of the same coin: if we are in danger of losing touch with the more transcendent aspirations of romance, it is exactly because we are taught to worship relationality for it own sake; as I have been arguing, we are taught to believe that having a relationship is more significant than the quality of that relationship. This is why so many of us reconcile ourselves to halfhearted alliances, sometimes even assuming that these alliances are the only kind we have any realistic chance of attaining. In this manner, we preclude the possibility of ever finding anything different. One reason it is so important to learn to tolerate stretches of aloneness is that frequently this is the only way to forge an opening for genuinely inspired love affairs. I do not mean to contribute to our society's relegation of singleness to the debased antechamber of marriage, for I stand by the idea that sometimes the best way to cultivate a depth of self-experience is to steer clear of relationships altogether. Yet I also think that there is nothing that makes it more impossible to discover the kind of love that is actually worth having than being so afraid of solitude that we hesitate to leave the safe but apathetic alliance we have sentenced ourselves to. In other words, if I want us to stop overvaluing relationships, it is in part because I would like us to stay receptive to ones whose value is indisputable—beyond the usual arithmetic of pros and cons, of logic and illogic.

6

The Ethics of Responsibility

We are responsible for what we cannot and do not control.
—Kelly Oliver

1

In the previous two chapters, I examined the manner in which our personal "fate," including the quality of our intimate relationships, is to some extent dictated by unconscious motivations that always remain somewhat inscrutable. This issue raises some difficult questions about interpersonal ethics, for it is not immediately obvious how we can take responsibility for what, to use Kelly Oliver's concise wording, "we cannot and do not control."[1] What do we do, for instance, when the truth of our desire clashes with the desires of others? And how do we respond to situations where the demons of our past drive us to hurt others in ways that we do not entirely understand? Are we less accountable for the impact of our behavior when it ensues from unconscious undercurrents we cannot contain? Can we excuse ourselves by claiming that it is our repetition compulsion that causes us to say unkind things or commit selfish actions?

As tempting as it might be to think so, I suspect this claim would let us off the hook too easily. It seems to me that if we repeatedly hurt others because of some archaic psychological or emotional blueprint, we are absolutely responsible for the pain we cause. I am of course by no means proposing that we will ever fully master this kind of radical responsibility. There will always be times when we speak or act before thinking. As a matter of fact, the more space we allow for the idiosyncrasies of our character, the more likely we are to slip in this manner, given that these idiosyncrasies to some extent circumvent the social conventions that mediate our relationships to others (more on this topic in the final section of this book). And it is obviously impossible for us to completely preempt our unconscious demons. But there is a difference between an occasional blunder and a prolonged pattern of wounding behavior. If we consistently injure others in the same way, we cannot very well hide behind the idea that our statements and actions are propelled by uncontrollable forces; we cannot disavow our responsibility to others by recourse to the idea that we do not know what we are doing.

Neither can we resort to the notion, common in many New Age approaches, that how others feel in a given interpersonal situation has little to do with what we say or do but reflects their self-undermining interpretation of the situation. This line of reasoning grows, in part at least, from the long-standing self-help motto—articulated in various ways by the field's heavyweights such as Wayne Dyer, Dr. Phil, Deepak Chopra, Louisa Hay, and Rhonda Byrne—that we can change our lives by changing the way we think. "Positive thinking," we are told, is the secret to a happy life. There may be some truth to this statement in the sense that the more optimistic we are, the more easily we might be able to recuperate from hardships and disillusionments. And I agree that the way we understand our lives can make a big difference in how these lives turn out, which is exactly why I have placed so much importance on the desirability of breaking painful repetition compulsions. But

I balk at the idea that thinking positive thoughts can change the objective circumstances of our lives, so that we can, say, think ourselves out of poverty or attain some cherished goal by tirelessly visualizing our triumph. There is, for example, something rather chilling about Byrne's claim, in her runaway best-seller *The Secret*, that we should be able to "attract" good things, including wealth, to ourselves by the sheer power of our thinking,[2] for it implies that those who have not been able to achieve the things that they want have somehow not tried hard enough—that ultimately those who fall through the cracks of the socioeconomic power structure have only themselves to blame. This ideology is an extreme version of the American dream that dictates that you should be able to accomplish just about anything as long as you put your mind to it.[3] Try telling that to the unemployed inner-city youth undergoing gang initiations, the "illegal aliens" picking oranges in California, the young boys and girls caught up in international sex-trafficking rings, the millions who go to bed hungry every night, or those living in war-torn regions of the world.

There is a certain absurdity to the idea that we can change our circumstances by positive thinking alone. And there is a related absurdity to the idea that our suffering is invariably of our own making, so that if others wound us, it is because we choose to read their statements or actions in wounding ways. To put the matter bluntly, there are plenty of situations where others actually say or do hurtful things—where our pain is not the outcome of our flawed interpretative processes, but of the bad behavior of others. This is easiest to see in the context of collective problems, so that it would, for instance, be ridiculous to fault the target of racism or sexism for his or her hurt feelings. In more intimate settings, things may get a bit blurrier, but if we reduce the notion that each of us is the author of our own suffering to its bare bones, it bears a striking resemblance to the outlook of abusive individuals who like to shift blame from themselves to their victims. A man who habitually mistreats his girlfriend may accuse her of overreacting. A father who routinely denigrates his daughter may tell her that her reactions are "hysterical." And a schoolyard bully who terrorizes a fellow pupil may add insult to injury by telling his crying prey that he is a pathetic weakling. In such instances, the abusive individual focuses on the reactions of the one who has been hurt rather than on his or her own behavior, with the result that responsibility becomes located within the injured party rather than within the perpetrator. Likewise with the idea that our suffering has nothing to do with the brutality of others but, rather, arises from our own mental processes.

I know that those who advocate this idea do not mean to endorse interpersonal cruelty. Their aim typically is to empower us so that we do not let the behavior of others determine our responses. Clearly, it is true that the more we recognize that our feelings, to a degree, are self-generated, the easier it becomes for us to fend off hurtful external influences. The problem, however, is threefold. First, this way of thinking can be argued to be a convenient means of promoting an extreme version of rugged individualism— a version that tells us to "grin and bear it" no matter how others conduct themselves—in the guise of self-development. Second, because it can cause us to blame ourselves for things that are not actually our fault, it can make us overly tolerant of others' insensitive attitudes. Third—and worst of all—when we flip it around, it explicitly invites us to renounce our responsibility for our *own* behavior. After all, if we believe that others get hurt not because of what we say or do, but because of how they interpret our statements and actions, what is to prevent us from saying or doing whatever the hell we please? In other words, there is nothing easier than manipulating this philosophy to our advantage by telling ourselves that if others get upset, it is because they are not mature (or "enlightened") enough to grasp that they are the origin of their own pain.

2

It is simply not true that human beings are always the sole cause of their own feelings. As I have shown, we are intrinsically open to the world, including other people, so that there is no way for any of us to ever completely ward off the pain of interpersonal callousness. To pretend otherwise is to deny something very basic about our foundational vulnerability. Granted, we can find ways to reduce this vulnerability. We can build psychological and emotional (and sometimes even physical) fortifications that to some extent protect us against the poisonous arrows aimed at us; we can develop a hard carapace that allows us to shrug off setbacks, difficulties, and disappointments as well as the hurtful words and actions of others. Alternatively—and perhaps more productively—we can learn various spiritual practices that mute the world's wounding impact. But the price we pay for this is that the more effective our defenses, the less we are able to participate in the art of fashioning a life that feels meaningful to us, for this art—as I hope to have demonstrated—by definition entails letting the world in. It is not just that we cannot exclude the bad without excluding the good. It is also that if we dodge the bad stuff, we cannot engage in the Nietzschean alchemy of transmuting life's adversities into existential openings; we cannot fully enter into the task of becoming the poets of our lives.

Conversely, I trust that most of us have enough emotional intelligence to know when we are behaving hurtfully. Unless we suffer from some sort of a clinical impairment of our emotional capacities, we understand the difference between respectful and disrespectful conduct and know when we are saying or doing things that are offensive, uncaring, or aggressive. It may be that there are situations where we cannot quite help ourselves—where we find ourselves speaking or acting in heartless ways despite our awareness that this is what we are doing. But this is different from the idea that we do not *realize* what we are doing. The fact that we sometimes inadvertently fall into hurtful interpersonal dynamics does not mean that we do not recognize the implications of our behavior. And it certainly does not absolve us of all accountability for it. This is why I think that the rhetoric that shifts the spotlight to the person on the receiving end of wounding conduct is often merely an expedient way to evade having to accept responsibility for one's words and actions.

Without doubt, there are times when we hurt others in ways we could not have prophesied. Because so much of human interaction involves unconscious trigger points, we cannot always foresee how our words and actions will be received by others. Sometimes we may even humiliate them by walking into an ancient but well-camouflaged minefield of mortification we did not realize existed; because the heartache of others is always highly singular, we cannot always keep ourselves from adding to it. But much of the time we can to some extent predict how our conduct will affect others. Although our predictions are never entirely accurate, in most instances we can arrive at a rough estimate of how our behavior will resonate within the inner lives of others. The more we are willing to admit this, the more possible it becomes for us to make better interpersonal choices. Furthermore, there is nothing to prevent us from offering restitution after the fact; because most of us do possess the capacity to recognize when we have said or done something questionable, there is no good excuse for not making amends (by apologizing, for example). But this kind of self-responsibility requires us to "own" our personal history—including the unconscious scripts that result from that history—in exactly the way I have outlined in this book; it asks us to become more discerning about how the unconscious impulses that we have inherited from our past guide our behavior in the present.

3

This manner of looking at things clashes fairly drastically with yet another idea that has in recent years leapt off the self-help shelf into the general population, namely that we should strive to live fully in the "now."[4] I would like to pause at this idea because it admittedly offers a viable alternative to the broadly therapeutic attitude I have taken in this book. I can certainly understand its appeal. It is true that we often accomplish nothing by dwelling on the past. And if this past contains a great deal of suffering, we can even harm ourselves by revisiting it too obsessively; we can retraumatize ourselves by incessantly reliving its traumas. I thus agree that there is much to be said for being able to shed the burdens of the past in order to embrace the present. Moreover, in the final chapter of this book, I outline an erotics of being that is also based on the notion of appreciating the now. I am therefore not trying to deny the potential richness of the present moment. Nor am I advocating excessive faithfulness to the past, let alone suggesting that we should reconcile ourselves to its painful legacies without any effort to work through these legacies. My point is rather that there is rarely a pure present that lasts longer than a fleeting moment. And it is also—and here I return to an argument I made in chapter 4—that we cannot banish the past by willpower alone, that we cannot simply "decide" that we won't let it get to us. Because we are not born anew every morning, because the past will always in one way or another be a part of the present, there can be no question of ridding ourselves of it in any unqualified sense. There is only the decision of how we are going to relate to it.

I have illustrated that when we bury (or exile or ignore or sideline) our past, we cannot help but repeat it (this is what is meant by the return of the repressed). In a way, we keep "remembering" on the unconscious level what we refuse to remember on the conscious one, with the result that our unconscious demons become all the more voracious. Moreover, when we abdicate our awareness of these demons, we also abdicate our influence over them so that we are much less prepared to deal with them when they take us by surprise (as they inevitably will). In contrast, when we remain cognizant of the historically driven character of our behavior, we become capable of intervention. We become capable of saying: "On second thought, I won't say what I was about to say. I won't act the way I was going to. I won't do so because I recall that when I did so in the past, it didn't have good consequences. I ended up hurting a person I cared about. And ultimately I gained nothing. I have learned my lesson and refuse to repeat the blunders of my past." This kind of reasoning is an essential component not only of our attempts to break our repetition compulsions, but also of thoughtful interpersonal conduct, which is precisely why I think that the idea of living fully in the now can be ethically quite confusing. To the extent that it underestimates the power of the past to shape our behavior in the present, it can keep us from recognizing how we might unconsciously, without meaning to, be pulling others into hurtful webs of relating that originate from our personal history.

Let us consider the issue from the point of view of memory. I am the first to admit that there are times when the best way to overcome something hurtful about the past is to become so passionate about the present that we simply just forget (and therefore automatically let go of) the past.[5] Generally speaking, if we were not able to forget some aspects of our history, we would quickly become oversaturated, filled with too many memories, too many recollections. According to this account, forgetting is essential for the continuation of life: it creates space for fresh experiences and thus, eventually, for fresh recollections. It allows us to desire new people, new goals and ambitions, new ideals and aspirations, which is to say, new existential possibilities. Without it, we would find it impossible to access the space of invention or discovery, for our devotion to the past would guarantee that our present would be merely a replica of this past. In this sense, an excess of memory can be the antithesis of life, whereas acts of forgetting can become a means of redrawing the sketch of our existence.

Yet, from a different perspective, forgetting can also be a sign of irresponsibility. This is easiest to understand on the collective level. There are situations where forgetting something or someone amounts to betraying them. For instance, forgetting social horrors such as slavery, the Holocaust, Hiroshima, Stalin's camps, apartheid, contemporary ethnic cleansings, or the mass rapes of women that have sometimes accompanied such cleansings would not only be disrespectful to the victims of these atrocities, but also unwise in making it impossible for us to accurately assess the lingering effects of the past on the present. We know that those living with the legacies of these events—and others like them—cannot possibly be unaffected by them and that it is consequently important for all of us, collectively, to hold onto the memory of these legacies. And we also know that the only way to escape repeating the mistakes of the past is to make sure that we do not forget about them (so that we recognize when something similar is happening or about to happen in the present). In such contexts, it would be almost obscene to forget, for doing so would imply that we rate our peace of mind higher than the fates of those who were killed, tortured, violated, or otherwise humiliated during such cruelties. Acts of remembrance, in contrast, are acts of fidelity: an ethical device for sustaining a vestige of events that we might otherwise feel tempted to erase from our consciousness.

Once we comprehend this connection, we can see that similar demands of fidelity may be made on us on a more personal level—that sometimes it is our responsibility to remember even when forgetting would be easier. Through our memory, we keep alive people from our past who would otherwise fall into oblivion. And we recall experiences that we cannot afford to forget because doing so would make it too easy for us to replicate our missteps. Indeed, one reason I find the attempt to translate the ideal of living fully in the present into a general philosophy of life so shortsighted is that it seems to voluntarily squander the wisdom of the past. It overlooks the fact that we can learn from the past so as to live more astutely (and therefore less destructively) in the present. And it also overlooks the fact that we possess the ability to read the past from the perspective of our current needs so that, as I have been proposing, we can make use of this past to better meet these needs. This is precisely why it is sometimes possible for us to transform a debilitating past into a more inspired modality of living. Our present, so to speak, conjures up the relevant elements of the past—the elements that have the potential to make a contribution to the present—in order to devise a new (and more rewarding) version of the present. This is one of the many ways in which we sustain ourselves as creatures of continuous becoming, as creatures who are capable of revising the framework of their lives.

4

Inasmuch as the ideal of living fully in the now jettisons the insights of the past for the sake of a harmonious present, it bankrupts the present, flattening our lives by depriving us of the complex history that has made us who we are. It starts from the mistaken premise that the more we manage to evacuate the present of any traces of the past, the more we will be able to transcend this past. What I have been arguing in this book is the exact opposite: that it is only by remaining keenly alert to the continued relevance of the past that we can keep it from controlling the contours of the present. Obviously, this is not always easy. Obviously, it takes a great deal of courage to accept the weight of the past in this manner and nowhere more so than in the context of relationships. Yet the fact that we have a self only because of others—that our personal viability, as well as the development of our character, depend on the presence of others—demands that we do so. It makes us fundamentally responsible for how we treat others, and this responsibility reaches beyond the conscious world of moral deliberation to the muddled underworld of our unconscious passions.

As long as we assume that we cannot be held accountable for what our unconscious compels us to do, our self-responsibility remains incomplete. Equally important, I believe that we have the right to expect similar accountability from others. I call attention to this right because there can be a great deal of pressure on us to forgive others for their indiscretions; we are often urged to be lenient with others when they lie to us, cheat on us, betray us, or insult us. To take a banal example: straight women are repeatedly told that they should be indulgent with men's slippages because men supposedly can't help themselves. Men, our relationship "experts" assure us, are "wired" to stray, act immaturely, fail at basic emotional intelligence, and overlook meaningful anniversaries. I hope that my discussion this far clarifies why I am not inclined to buy any of this argument. I do not think that the idea of being (biologically or otherwise) "wired" to hurt women is any more convincing than the idea that we hurt others because our unconscious "makes" us do so. It merely provides a convenient rationalization for brutish behavior, which is why I am so baffled by self-help authors who cheerily feed women this line of logic. What exactly, besides continued subordination and interpersonal wretchedness, do women have to gain from the deeply patriarchal, traditionalist mentality that dominates contemporary relationship advice? Why should any woman settle for a caveman version of masculinity when there are plenty of emotionally savvy and respectful men in the world?

If I am going to hold myself accountable for my behavior even when it is unconsciously motivated, I am not going to let others get away with insensitive conduct simply because they tell me that they cannot restrain themselves. To be sure, our awareness of the ways in which we are not transparent to ourselves—of the ways in which our unconscious demons sometimes drive us to offend others against our better judgment—should make us patient with the ethical lapses of others. It should lead to a kind of solidarity of vulnerability whereby we understand that in the same way that we are partially incomprehensible to ourselves, others are also incomprehensible to themselves. In the same way that we sometimes find ourselves carried by mysterious impulses we cannot entirely decode, others find themselves overtaken by enigmatic passions they cannot easily defuse. In the same way that we are always a bit startling, a bit strange and perplexing, to ourselves, others can experience themselves as profoundly decentered. And in the same way that we can be tormented by our memories, others can be mired in painful recollections; in exactly the same way that we occasionally let the past get the better of us, others occasionally let the past get the better of them, with the result that they wound us. But none of this means that the people we interact with are not responsible for their behavior.

5

Let us unpack this notion of responsibility more carefully. None of us can monitor every aspect of our being. And none of us can fully account for how we have become who we are.[6] Many of our most formative experiences take place so early in our lives that they fade away before we get a chance to grasp the role they have played in our development. This is why the batter of which we are made always contains ingredients we do no know about. Furthermore, some of the clandestine forces that guide our behavior can be quite disorderly—and sometimes even vehemently disobedient—so that they grate against our wish for self-consistency; they stick out of and disturb the coherence of our identity, with the consequence that there are times when we may even feel a little terrorized by our own potential for unruliness. The same applies to others. What is universally true of human beings is that we all are to some degree alien to ourselves. As singular as each of us is, what we share with each other is the reality of never completely "coinciding" with ourselves in the sense that the self that is thinking and feeling at any given moment cannot possibly remain conscious of, let alone contain, all the conflicting energies of its constitution. Knowing that other people are just as inundated by this type of existential uncertainty as we are places specific kinds of demands on our ethical attitude toward them—demands that our customary codes of relationality are not necessarily very good at addressing.

Some contemporary critics, such as Slavoj Žižek, have posited that our tendency to feel threatened by the more volatile, rebellious dimensions of others means that an ethics based on empathy and interpersonal identification is inherently fallacious. According to Žižek, such an ethics relies on the assumption that we can treat the other as a "fellow human being," as someone "just like us," when in fact we have no foundation for positing such a platform of commonality.[7] As a matter of fact, we can erect this platform only by sidelining everything about the other that is not compatible with our inherited conception of what it means to be a human being. This is exactly why our empathy tends to falter the moment the other no longer makes sense to us, the moment he or she deviates from our understanding of what constitutes reasonable human conduct, as is the case, for instance, when we are confronted by a suicide bomber, a religious fanatic, or someone else whose actions do not correspond to our definition of acceptable behavior; our well-meaning rhetoric of tolerance, ironically enough, flounders in the face of those who seem fiercely intolerant.[8] On this view, our biggest ethical challenge is not how we might be able to build a viable "human" community out of drastically different personal and cultural values, but rather how we might be able meet what seems most "inhuman," most "monstrous" (to use one of Žižek's favorite terms), about the other.

A related formulation—one that Žižek also emphasizes—is the question of how we might be able to meet the suffering of someone who has been so thoroughly dehumanized that he or she has been divested of all signs of personal vitality or individuality. Such a person is ethically disquieting not because of her own actions, but rather because of the mark of anguish that the radical violence of others has left on her. Žižek's example of such utter destitution is the concentration camp inmate—whom Giorgio Agamben has evocatively characterized as a *Muselmann*: a mere shell of a man.[9] Žižek claims that our customary ethical attitude collapses when we are confronted by such a spectacle of dehumanization, by such a "faceless" face.[10] This vacant, impassive face is no longer a socially intelligible face, which is exactly why it stretches the limits of our aptitude for empathy and identification. As such, it stands for the limit case of "humanity" by persisting as a material presence in the absence of all conventional signifiers of relational capacity. Because it cannot be easily assimilated into the cadence of our emotional universe, we, quite simply, do not know what to do with it. Indeed, all manner of response seems atrociously inadequate, which is why we often feel pathetically helpless in the aftermath of sadistic scenes of cruelty and degradation.

These two examples reference two very different instances of ethical failure, but both have to do with our understanding of the parameters of humanity. The first highlights the difficulty of seeing the human (or humane) in those whose values are fundamentally different from ours; the second points to instances where the other has been so completely broken that the abyss of her suffering seems to have devoured her humanity. As a result, both highlight the fact that our traditional ethical models fail to reach the potentially traumatizing core of ethics. Because such models routinely bypass relational scenarios that either test the boundaries of our open-mindedness or bring us so close to the edge of abjection that our capacity for compassion begins to fray, they do not confront what is genuinely difficult about intersubjective responsibility. Or, to state the matter slightly differently, insofar as these models rely on ideals of empathy and identification that function by translating what is unfamiliar into something seemingly familiar, they deny the irreducible otherness, the impenetrable alterity, of the other, thereby committing ethical violence at the precise moment when they pretend to act ethically. All of this suggests that a properly ethical attitude should be able to risk an encounter with what is most uncanny about the other; it should be able to meet those aspects of the other that cannot be integrated into the usual rhythm of interpersonal exchange, negotiation, and communication. This is not the same thing as saying that we should never judge others— as I argue later, there are times when we must. But it implies that ethics as an attitude of relationality is much more tenuous, much more prone to malfunction, than we are accustomed to think.

6

Yet it is also possible to overplay the difficulty. Although I agree with the general thrust of Žižek's arguments, I am not entirely persuaded that understanding others, or empathizing with their plight, is always as hard as Žižek makes it out to be. I am not even altogether convinced that ethically responding to the dehumanization of the *Muselmann* is impossible. Though it would be preposterous to assert that those of us who have not been incarcerated can fully identify with the experiences of a concentration camp survivor, let alone that our empathy alone can ever redeem what happened, it may be equally problematic to claim that we are completely incapable of approaching this survivor from a place of genuine concern. It seems to me that there is an important difference between, on the one hand, acknowledging the limits of our capacity for empathy and, on the other, abandoning all efforts to connect with the agony of others because we deem them to be hopeless. The fact that we cannot ever entirely comprehend the other's experience does not mean that we cannot comprehend *something* about it, that we remain completely exiled from the other's private universe. Likewise, the fact that our powers of compassion may falter when confronted by the raw realities of the other's pain in no way implies that we cannot kindly touch some portion of that pain. One of the dangers of insisting on the disquieting aspects of the other is that it can eclipse the fact that, ultimately, we have a great deal in common with each other—that the other who is unknowable is always also in some ways knowable.

I suspect that when people claim that they have no way of accessing the emotional world of others, it is not always necessarily because the task is impossible, but because they are reluctant to try hard enough; they are unwilling to make the effort of bridging the gap between their own singularity and that of another person. Though it may be that this gap is always to some degree unbridgeable— that our systems of interpersonal comparison will always remain defective—it is rarely the case that we are completely incapable of understanding where others are coming from. As a consequence, when we declare that someone's experience is "too different" from ours, what we usually mean is that we cannot be bothered to work our way beyond the discrepancies between self and other. Against this backdrop, it might help to focus less on the other's disconcerting "monstrousness" than on what we share with him or her. This is exactly what Judith Butler has done in her attempt to develop an ethics based on universal human precariousness: the recognition that we all are susceptible to injury at the hands of others.[11] Such vulnerability is of course unequally disseminated so that—as I have been suggesting throughout this book—some lives are much more precarious than others. In effect, the vast power differentials of the world target some populations for precariousness while safeguarding others against it, so that how we are positioned in relation to global, national, communal, or familial support systems determines how fragile our lives are, practically speaking. But, in principle, the *potential* for precariousness is what unites us as human beings, and it is our awareness of this potential that, according to Butler, gives us the ethical tools for relating to the suffering of others.

Our awareness that the other is as woundable as we are represents, for Butler, a precious ethical resource in the sense that it offers a starting point for our indignation, outrage, and horror in the face of any and all violence committed against the other. On this view, we oppose injustice done to the other because, on some level, we can place ourselves in the other's position—because we perceive that, under different conditions, the oppression aimed at the other, or at least something akin to this oppression, could be aimed at us. Moreover, knowing that the other shares our existential disorientation goes a long way in making us more tolerant of his or her mishaps and errors of judgment; it goes a long way in helping us "understand" the other even if we do not always understand his or her motivations. This is exactly why I noted earlier that the fact that we are not fully transparent to ourselves should give rise to the kind of solidarity of vulnerability that acknowledges that the other can be just as confused about his or her choices as we sometimes are about ours. As much as we might (rightly) worry about the ethical pitfalls of using the self as a point of comparison, it is also the case that we are capable of meaningful relationality in part precisely because we are able to detect the similarities between self and other, because we can often (not always, but often) assume a measure of psychological and emotional symmetry.

This dynamic obviously works only to the degree that we are able to see the other in the first place—to the degree that we have access to some representation, however inadequate, of the other's lived reality. This is why Butler has asserted that, on the global scale, the problem is that our habitual frames of perception—ones that are strongly influenced by what our media choose to show us—can render some individuals, some populations, invisible, so that we no longer recognize their suffering as valid, let alone as something that concerns us. Our grief cannot reach such individuals, such populations, for the simple reason that our political system and its army of media minions meddle with our ability to see them as fully human.[12] Under extreme conditions, such as war, we may even come to think of them as "evil," as lacking in basic human decency, because we need to be able to justify our violence toward them. In such situations, our ability to mourn the anguish of others is blocked because we lack the necessary grounds for empathy and interpersonal affinity. Indeed, if it is the case, as I have been proposing, that we tend to lose our ethical stance of generosity whenever we are no longer capable of identifying with the existential struggles of others, then war and other scenarios of violence are designed to sever that identification; they are designed to grind down our outrage at the torment of others so that we can ignore this torment with a good conscience. If the propaganda machine of war invariably seeks to paint the enemy as less than human, it is because it is easier to kill (or torture) what in no way resembles the self.

7

Ethics would not be such a wrought notion if our relationship to others were always comfortable. The real ethical dilemma arises when we are asked to be charitable vis-à-vis those who make us anxious or defensive. This is why it is imperative to look for the kernel of humanity in those who seem most devoid of it. And it is also why it is important to be patient with those who defy our comprehension. This, however, should not be confused with the idea that others are not responsible for their actions when they treat us poorly. Butler sometimes speaks as if human opacity were an automatic ticket to forgiveness, as if the existential disorientation of those we interact with somehow absolved them of all accountability for their behavior. And she seems to advocate a similar leniency with ourselves whenever we slip and do something we did not mean to. As she claims, "I will need to be forgiven for what I cannot have fully known, and I will be under a similar obligation to offer forgiveness to others, who are also constituted in partial opacity to themselves."[13] To some degree, I understand her position. But I also think that it needs serious qualification.

On the one hand, as Arendt has pointed out, many of our actions are inherently risky in that they have unpredictable and irreversible consequences. Because we cannot ever quite foresee how a given deed is going to play itself out in the world, and particularly because we cannot undo it even when its effects are disastrous, we are always to some extent fallible. The only remedy for this predicament is the forgiveness of others; the only thing that saves us from a paralysis of inaction—that allows us to begin anew after we have blundered—is our hope that others will forgive our trespasses.[14] Kelly Oliver has expanded on this view by asserting that one of the inequalities of our collective world is that those who hold positions of power are forgiven for their transgressions more readily than those who are disempowered.[15] In other words, those with privilege get to celebrate their socially disruptive singularity, whereas those who lack it are persecuted for even the slightest eruption of theirs. In part, this is because those on top of the pyramid of authority understand that the most effective way for the socially marginalized to improve their lot might be a violent uprising of some kind. In the same way that a mutiny of slaves can succeed only at the expense of the slave owners, and a revolution can succeed only at the expense of the reigning government, the downtrodden may feel as if there were no option but to stage a rebellion that attacks the hegemonic establishment that oppresses them. In such situations, withholding forgiveness for transgressions (or for displays of singularity) is a means of keeping the disempowered in line, which in turn implies that choosing to cultivate a degree of forbearance toward their infractions might be an act of political solidarity.

On the other hand, it would be difficult to make the same argument about a serial killer who targets a specific type of victim, a military mission that degenerates into a needless bloodbath, a racist mob that attacks an immigrant, a homophobic gang that brutalizes a gay man, or even a cruel husband who crushes his wife's self-esteem on a daily basis. Such people may have their reasons: they may come from backgrounds that taught them to act this way; they may have suffered a great deal so that their violence is a misguided attempt to translate their pain into something more manageable; or they may be goaded by some obscure inner urge that they cannot comprehend. But if we accept these reasons as an excuse, we rate their torment higher than that of their victims. This is, among other things, why I have placed so much weight on the idea that unconscious inclinations—even ones that draw their energy from devastating pasts—are not exempt from the demands of self-responsibility. Furthermore, people often hurt others not because of their inner opacity or even out of thoughtlessness, but because of a hunger for power, a sense of superiority, or a predilection for contempt. Forgiving them too easily would amount to condoning their actions; it would amount to rewarding them for interpersonal brutality.

We routinely make life-shaping decisions without having all the facts. But this does not absolve us of responsibility for our choices. For instance, if I am a medical student who harms a patient because I minister the wrong dose of a dangerous drug, I may garner some sympathy from those who understand my predicament. But I will still be held accountable. Why, then, should things be any different with our inner opacities and unconscious motivations? The fact that there is a degree of murkiness and unfreedom at the core of our lives does not mean that we have no clarity or freedom at all. It merely means that this clarity or freedom is never unconditional—and that sometimes we need to work quite hard to attain it. In this context, it might be helpful to recall that when Freud urged us to explore our unconscious lives, he certainly did not mean that we should resign ourselves to self-indulgent impotence. Rather, he wanted us to gain more awareness of how our unconscious habits structure our world, including our relational world, so that we can make better choices about how we interact with this world. More specifically, he wanted us to understand that our missteps are not always random and that a greater measure of self-reflexivity can consequently keep us from repeatedly hurting ourselves and others. Obviously, we cannot always succeed at this task, but this hardly means that we should abandon the effort to do so. And I think that we can expect similar effort, similar accountability, from others even when we might simultaneously empathize with their ongoing struggle to assume the considerable burden of that effort and accountability.

All of this brings us to a very thorny question—namely, how we are to reconcile our existential bewilderment with the need for universal principles of justice. After all, even if we all share this bewilderment, its idiosyncratic manifestations tend to be so mutually conflicting that they drive a wedge between self and others, making it harder to establish common ground. There are many who have responded to this impasse by asserting that universal ethical codes are not only untenable, but deeply undesirable. I understand this verdict in the sense that I know that, historically speaking, what has been deemed "universal" has often been merely the point of view of the socially privileged. That is, those who have held culturally dominant positions have been able to dictate the precincts of "universality," so that the concept has lost much of its credibility and, even worse, excluded many people who did not seem to fall within its borders. At the same time, without some notion of universally applicable ethical codes, it is difficult to check the abuses of power; it is difficult to keep displays of idiosyncrasy from sliding into the anarchy of the (physically or socioeconomically) strongest. This is why I continue to believe in the importance of universal justice even as I am well aware of its historical failings. As I see it, such failings do not topple the entire ideal of universality, but merely reveal that we have not yet been able to devise a genuinely universal version of this ideal; we have not been able to dissociate our concept of universality from the realities of social power. It may well be that we will never fully accomplish this feat—that the universal will always to some extent be tainted by power. But I hope we can make some progress.

There are times when we need to make decisions about right and wrong and to act accordingly. Whether we are talking about a man aiming his gun at Norwegian youth or about a dictator aiming his genocidal rage at segments of his own population, we need universally applicable principles—normative limits—and the fact that we might never be able to agree entirely on their parameters does not diminish the urgency of our desperate need for them. What I have attempted to illustrate in this chapter is that our unconscious quirks are not beyond the domain of normative limits, that we cannot use them as an excuse for bad behavior. Quite the contrary, we can only become fully ethical beings when we accept responsibility for them, when we recognize that they are as much a part of who we are as our more conscious attributes. This is why I have proposed that our art of living stays sadly superficial as long as it fails to activate the unconscious frequencies of our being; it is why I have aligned the crafting of character with the ability not only to work through but also to become answerable for the hungry demons that lie in wait in the obscure corners of our interiority. Inner opacity, on this account, is not a pretext for interpersonal violence, but an invitation to a more far-reaching form of relational ethics; it is not a justification for wounding behavior, but a call to greater ethical vigilance—the kind of vigilance that acknowledges that we are not nearly as feeble in relation to our unconscious motivations as we sometimes might like to think.

PART III

THE ART OF
SELF-SURRENDER

7

The Swerve of Passion

Love what you will never believe twice.

—Alain Badiou

1

This far I have focused on processes of self-fashioning that allow us to cultivate our character as well as on genres of self-experience that allow us to take responsibility for that character. But there is another way to understand what it means to hear the call of our character, and it takes us in the seemingly opposite direction of self-surrender. I say *seemingly* because the final section of this book is devoted to illustrating that self-surrender can be an essential component of self-fashioning—that there are times when the most effective way to access our character is to suspend the relatively organized structure of our identity by letting ourselves fall into a less organized state of being. In the chapters that follow, I present some ways to think about this in the context of everyday life. But first I want to examine what is perhaps the most thrilling aspect of this alternative way of approaching our theme—namely, those moments when we feel called to a new destiny so powerfully that we have no choice but to obey. During such moments, we are assailed by what might best be characterized as a "swerve of passion": a sudden upsurge of passion that overpowers, and sometimes even erases, our usual sources of passion. Such a swerve disrupts our normal existential rhythm, asking us to redraw the basic outline of our lives in ways that leave little room for negotiation or second-guessing. As a result, it is as terrifying as it is exhilarating, which is why the temptation to betray it is ever present. Yet to the degree that we betray it, we betray our character.

The fastest entry point to our topic is the work of the contemporary philosopher Alain Badiou.[1] Badiou proposes that our lives consist of two different levels. The first is the mundane domain of personal interests and concerns, our daily "business as usual." The second is the domain of what he calls the "event": an unexpected flash of insight that alters our entire life orientation. Such an event overtakes us suddenly, without warning. It can be as lofty as an artistic innovation, a scientific discovery, or a political epiphany. Or it can be as ordinary as falling in love. The point is that it shatters the shell of our usual preoccupations, sending us in life directions that we might not have been able to foresee. It radically changes our customary manner of looking at things, making visible what remains invisible from within the status quo of our lives. It reveals aspects of our reality that we are not used to seeing, perhaps because we have been too afraid to take a good look or because we have been too busy with other parts of our lives to notice. It, in short, invites us to place our faith in the exceptional rather than in the expected, which is why Badiou urges us to love what we would "never believe twice."[2] Such love of the singular, Badiou specifies, is the opposite of loving only what we have always believed to be true.

The event is the improbable, hard-to-imagine occurrence that nevertheless, miraculously, manages to occur. It reverses a previously held view so that we are able to assess things differently. Most important, it spurs us to the kind of action that we never thought we were capable of. This is how political revolutionaries are born. And it is how artists, scientists, and other creative individuals get caught up in a burning passion that compels them to pour all of their energies into their undertaking. For those of us who do not possess the political or creative spark, falling in love may be the closest we ever come to a genuine event in Badiou's sense, which is one reason I argued earlier that love should not be confused with the lukewarm conveniences of cohabitation. The sensation of being swept off our feet by love is a concrete way to grasp what Badiou means when he maintains that the event represents an eruption of insight that makes it impossible for us to proceed with our lives as usual. It demands our willingness to reorganize our entire manner of being in accordance to the message we have received. And it asks us to honor its directive even though we have no way of knowing whether we will succeed in the end, whether we will manage to realize the artistic, scientific, political, or amorous ideal that has caught us by the throat.

Badiou is merely the latest in a long list of philosophers, mystics, writers, and artists to investigate a phenomenon that, for many, represents the culmination of human existence: the experience of being summoned to a higher "calling"—a vocation, purpose, or prophetic revelation beyond our normal way of going about our lives. Such a calling jolts us out of our complacency, seizes our entire being, and makes us single-mindedly preoccupied by the insight we have been granted. This is why Plato talked about the lover as a madman so mesmerized by the beauty of the beloved that he is unable to attend to any of his usual tasks, why mystics talk about being penetrated by a messianic power that cannot be resisted, and why writers and artists talk about being overtaken by an inspiration that leaves them no alternative but to try to realize their vision. There may well be an acuteness to such a summons that transcends what most of us are able to achieve. But I think that anyone who has ever felt the thrill of new love or known the elation of creative "flow" has had a taste of what I am talking about. This taste, I would like to propose, is one of the most important ways in which we are called to our character. It is not the only way; but it is the most compelling.

2

I have emphasized all along that there is often a tension between our social persona and our character. Badiou's notion of the event brings this tension into sharp focus. If our social lives are composed of habits, routines, and to-do lists that carry us from one moment to the next, the singular event pushes us beyond the daily grind, beyond the monotony of our ordinary concerns, by offering us an acute reminder of the needs of our character. It activates that part of our being that has not been entirely tamed by the normative expectations of the social world. This part is looking for a "cause" of some kind. It wants to live vigorously and without hesitation. Perhaps most notably, it does not care about what everyone else thinks. It is not interested in cultural standards that tell us what we are supposed to believe, how we are supposed to act, and where we are supposed to look for satisfaction. It forms its own distinctive creed of beliefs, actions, and satisfactions without much regard for whether this creed corresponds to what the collective order considers right and proper.

Being called to our character in this manner rescues us from being entirely engulfed by conventional definitions of the good life. Simply put, the things that make us socially successful are often of little interest to our character, which is, by definition, a bit of a loner. It wants to do things in its own way. It does not mind creating ripples, for it is less concerned with what is expedient than with what is spellbinding and breathtaking. It is not even afraid to alienate those around us: because it does not worry about security or the approval of others, it is willing to sacrifice a lot of its social reputation. It acts without regard for consequences, sometimes tarnishing the public image that renders us culturally comprehensible—that makes us legible to others. This happens when we, for instance, abandon a promising career for another one that seems idiotically risky, replace a long-standing aspiration with one that seems completely unrealistic, or suddenly break all of our commitments in order to follow a new lover—someone we barely know—across the globe. In such instances, our actions may appear reckless and even a little insane to others, yet we sense that they possess their own internal validity. They cannot be judged by external criteria because they are incontestably "right" for us even if they are not right for others (and even if they cannot be rationally justified).

Let us think of the matter as follows. All of us have made certain kinds of investments in our lives. We have devoted ourselves to our education, careers, lovers, friends, bodies, hobbies, futures, and so on. Such investments tend to be strong, for they form the backbone of our existence. But when they become too habitual, too matter of fact, they can trap us in listless existential modalities. In contrast, when we are called to our character, we are unexpectedly "lifted" by a force that seems stronger than any of our usual investments. This force feels irresistible because it summons us to something "more than"—as Lacan might put it—the ordinary reality that we are living; it prods us toward the transcendent and uniquely inspired. This does not mean that it asks us to exchange the world for some sort of otherworldly domain. Quite the opposite, as I demonstrate in chapter 9, it teaches us to attain the transcendent within the creases of daily life, without ever leaving the world behind; it enables us to perceive the sumptuousness of the world so that the "worldly" no longer corresponds to what is mundane. The "worldly," then, is not the enemy, but rather the tiny steps of tedium that tend to take over our lives when we are not paying attention. The call of our character reminds us that when life gets reduced to such steps—when we get so focused on getting through the day that our habits, routines, and to-do lists swallow up our entire reality—it loses its luminosity, with the result that it also loses its creative thrust.

There is an obvious similarity between the act of staying loyal to the echo of the Thing that I discussed earlier and the experience of being called to our character that I am describing here: both introduce a code of conduct that deviates from the collective code that governs normative, socially anticipated behavior. As I have explained, when we interact with an object that contains the Thing's echo, we interact with both the object itself and the

Thing's sublime trace (what in the object is "more than" the object itself). This is why such an object makes us feel singularly galvanized, in temporary possession of something "more than" a common item of use. Likewise, the event electrifies us because it speaks directly to the part of us that longs for something "more than" our pragmatic preoccupations. In Badiou's terminology, it releases the "immortal" within our being. By this, Badiou does not mean that there is a component of us—say, a soul—that will never die, but rather that there is something within us that is not satisfied with our "mortal" (banal, everyday) concerns. This "immortal" yearns for the transcendent, the incandescent, which is exactly what the event delivers. The event reaches beyond the bounds of ordinary experience toward the extraordinary, which is why its summons is as exultant as it is obligatory.

3

The event demands our unconditional faithfulness, so that the worst we could do would be to betray it, be it through laziness, weakness, or complacency. It asks us to hold our ground even when the world offers resistance or even when it is filled with seductions—with alternative points of interest—that vie for our attention. The most obvious example of a situation where our faithfulness might be tested is a political commitment that requires the absolute dedication of its supporters regardless of cost to their personal well-being. But our fidelity might also waver in less explosive situations—for instance, when we are struggling to translate a creative inspiration into some sort of a concrete product or when we are forced to cope with the bouts of insecurity caused by a professional calling that does not organically follow from what we have done previously. Not only might we feel daunted by the enormity of the task, but those around us might try to convince us that our devotion is imprudent, that our inspiration or calling is an illusion that will take us in untenable or even harmful directions. Moreover, we might have important prior responsibilities to uphold—ones that it might be impossible to cast aside without doing some damage either to ourselves or to others. In such cases, staying faithful to our vision might require seemingly superhuman strength.

What is more, the challenge of faithfulness is not just a matter of honoring the event itself, but of sustaining its flash long after it has expired. When the doubts start creeping in—when the passage of time dilutes our initial enthusiasm and erodes our resolve—the temptation to revert to our familiar life of personal interests and concerns can be considerable. And what complicates matters even further is that our doubts are not even necessarily erroneous. There is always the possibility of being drastically wrong. It may be entirely true that we have allowed ourselves to be deluded by something that masquerades as a life-altering event, but that in reality is a mere illusion. This is why Badiou distinguishes between authentic events and simulacra. The latter are "events" that display all the outward characteristics of the genuine event yet turn out to be false in the sense that they do not lead us to anything inspired but merely feed our narrow-mindedness. Indeed, because narrow-mindedness, like the event, is fueled by passion, it is easy to confuse the two, which is why the most chilling of Badiou's examples of misleading simulacra are political upheavals—such as Hitler's rise to power—that elicit strong passions but do not serve a higher goal. The followers of Hitler exhibited the kind of single-minded fidelity that also characterizes those faithful to the genuine event. But their fidelity served the deadly force of prejudice rather than the life-affirming force of transcendent insight.

On a more prosaic level, our fidelity to a new inspiration or vocation may be misguided in the sense that this inspiration or vocation may not, upon closer inspection, merit our investment. It may at first seem to transmit the sublime ethos of a genuine event but later reveal itself to have been mere simulacrum (and therefore a waste of our energies). Along similar lines, the initial blush of infatuation may appear akin to "real" love even though it is fated to fade in a matter of months. That said, it is not the case that an inspiration, vocation, or love that does not last is *automatically* false. The fact that a given passion may over time exhaust itself does not necessarily mean that the passion was never authentic. I already made this point about love when I argued that it would be a mistake to think that only those of our relationships that endure are meaningful. But the same applies to other kinds of "events" as well. Even when they do not persist across time, they may leave behind effects that do. For instance, some of Da Vinci's inspirations may have been proven flawed, but this does not erase their world-transforming impact. As a matter of fact, even the emergence of new events—new epiphanies—does not always cancel out the importance of previous ones, as long as they were genuine events.

4

An event can thus turn out to be false. At the same time, an event that is supplanted by newer (and perhaps more "accurate") events may nevertheless remain true. Such complexity can make it difficult to determine which events are worthy of our fidelity and which are not. In other words, fidelity is inherently demanding because the destiny we feel summoned to remains shadowy: we cannot predict how things will turn out in the end. And, most vexingly, there is no way to tell ahead of time what is "real" and what is not. No wonder, then, that it can be hard to have faith that we will eventually reach our destination (and that this destination is actually worth reaching). It can be hard to trust that our calling is not just a glittery lure calculated to deceive us. And, perhaps most important, it can be hard to trust that we have enough strength to see things through. If even the most fervent revolutionaries sometimes lose their courage, and if even the most talented artists and scientists cannot always bring their revelations into a victorious conclusion, and if even the most ardent lovers at times give up on their passion for the sake of prudence, how can the rest of us possibly manage the disorienting aftermath of an event that turns our world upside down? Even when the event is clearly authentic, we may doubt our ability to sustain our fidelity to it, and for a good reason, for it is easy to get so exhausted or discouraged that the thought of going on fills us with trepidation.

The existential disarray caused by the event can grab us on such a visceral level that we find it difficult to proceed with the practical demands of daily life. On the one hand, responding to the event can release energies that have been trapped in false self-presentations and sometimes even in symptomatic fixations, so that new sources of life, new sources of joy, become available to us. In this sense, the event's impact is not unlike the impact of breaking a repetition compulsion. On the other hand, the sudden discharge of energy that accompanies the event can be destabilizing precisely because it interferes with our symptomatic fixations. As I have implied, if there is an "advantage" to our fixations, it is that, in their contorted way, they grant us a semblance of security. They lend structure to our lives, and even if this structure is debilitating, even if it hurts us, it may still feel easier to cope with than the complete lack of structure. In the same way that an obsessive who follows his or her routine feels better (at least temporarily) than one who is somehow prevented from doing so, we gain a degree of comfort from our symptoms; on some level, we appreciate our symptoms, which is one reason we tend to hold on to them with a degree of irrational tenacity. One of the challenges of the event is that it removes our pathological safety net. It asks us to detach our energies from our symptoms so that we can direct them to the unknown represented by the event. Needless to say, doing so can threaten the very underpinnings of our identity.

Navigating the combination of thrill and threat that characterizes the event can be extremely demanding. The urge to abandon our loyalty to it can be overpowering, particularly because we may find the thrill as difficult to manage as the threat. We are not, after all, used to living in a state of thrill. As elating as this state may be, it can also feel overstimulating to the point of agony. Think of artists who describe their moments of peak creativity as almost torturous. Or think of what it feels like when you cannot sleep because you are so in love with someone that you cannot stop thinking about him or her. It is as if we needed limits to our inspiration, and particularly to our enjoyment, in the sense that when it reaches a certain acuity, it becomes more or less unbearable. As much as we covet pleasurable experiences, we can sustain them only on a fairly modest level. When we are pushed over the edge, we land in anguish, which is one reason we are constantly looking for moderation in our lives. Unfortunately, moderation is the very antithesis of the event, for the event by definition carries an excess of both promise and agitation. It opens up a cauldron of new possibilities, but because it also forces us onto an unfamiliar terrain, these possibilities are always intertwined with the prospect of losing our footing, of becoming frighteningly unbalanced.

5

The difficulty of responding to the event with any degree of moderation explains, in part at least, the appeal of "reasonable" lives. When we live "reasonably," we live without excess passion or excess anguish. In contrast, when we allow ourselves to be summoned by an event, we stumble into a place where both passion and anguish threaten to spill over. This is exactly why the needs of our character and those of our social persona tend to clash. In the same way that it can sometimes be hard to reconcile love's sublimity with its more mundane aspects—that it can be hard to keep our everyday routine from eroding the more transcendent promises of romance—it can be difficult to foster the spirit of our character within our otherwise "reasonable" lives. I have suggested that the contrast between our character and our social persona mirrors the contrast between the event and the (personal or collective) status quo that the event destabilizes. This in turn implies that the more we side with our character, the less space we have left for the investments that support our social persona. Yet it is usually impossible for us to completely excuse ourselves from such investments. Nor would many of us want to, for even if these investments tend to guide us to conventional modes of living, they are often also among the most meaningful elements of our existence. In fact, some of them might be the consequence of prior events, prior personal epiphanies. After all, if—as I have claimed—the event leads to an unusually strong investment, then there is a good chance that at least some of our current investments started out as events. It might, for instance, be that a career path that does not seem particularly scintillating now was once a tremendous inspiration—that our mistake is not that we made the wrong investment, but that we have gradually allowed ourselves to lose track of its more enlivening dimensions.

Our choice, then, is not always between an event and a non-event, but rather between a new event and the (sometimes admittedly wilted) vestiges of an old one. As I specified earlier, the fact that an event does not survive over time does not necessarily make it false. Consequently, if it would be foolish to suppress the summons of a new event, it might be equally foolish to completely sacrifice the rest of our lives—including the remnants of older events that persist through our long-term investments—to this summons. Badiou's point about the (new) event, of course, is that its summons is so commanding that there is no room for deliberation: we have no choice but to heed its calling. But I can imagine situations where this summons is not quite so resounding, where we might be able to weigh our preexisting commitments against the new passion that is asking to be taken seriously. In saying this, I do not wish to retract my critique of personally or socially complacent paradigms of living, for I believe that such paradigms can anesthetize us to the point of existential stupor. But I want once again to be vigilant about dissociating this critique from the idea that all conventional investments are worthless. I suppose I would say that the problem is not that we have such investments, but that we routinely fail to differentiate between investments that continue to be compatible with the needs of our (ever-evolving) character and others that do not.

To state the issue concretely, allowing ourselves to be summoned out of a love affair that has become obsolete is entirely different from allowing ourselves to be summoned out of one that could use a little nudge but is still reasonably alive. Likewise, allowing ourselves to be called out of a career path that we experience as deadening is quite different from allowing ourselves to be called out of one that still contains enclaves of inspiration. This is why learning to accurately read the truth of our desire is so essential: when we remain confused about what most matters to us, we will not be able to distinguish between a summons that warrants a complete overhaul of our lives and another that is likely to lead us astray. As long as the voice that is telling us to break with our old commitments articulates a real (truthful) desire, it merits our attention no matter how irrational it may seem. But if it turns out that this voice is a simulacrum—that it does not reflect the authenticity of our desire, but merely the seductive sparkle of the decoys that colonize our life-world—following its calling would be an error of judgment. This is exactly why I have asserted that there is little that enhances our art of living more than being able to recognize the difference between objects (and activities) that contain the Thing's echo and others that do not; it is why I have stressed the importance of knowing when to invest our energies and when to hold back.

Moreover, there is no way around the fact that there are times when we need to strike a compromise between our idiosyncratic passions and our social investments. Though this compromise may appear like an instant betrayal—though it may be hard to translate the demands of our character into socially manageable morsels without thereby degrading their dignity—some amount of mediation tends to be necessary. Ideally, we should be able to find a means of weaving strands of eccentricity into our otherwise somewhat conventional lives. Although it would be self-serving to be overly focused on our character, we also cannot afford to lose track of it; we do not want to feel alienated from society, but neither do we want to be so seamlessly a part of it that we have no distinctive passions. As a matter of fact, when we lose our character in this manner, we lose not only what is singular about us, but also our capacity to take responsibility for ourselves; we lose our ability to make decisions independently of our surroundings so that we eventually become mere inert putty in the hands of the powers that be. In contrast, to the degree that we are able to incorporate some of the resistant energy of our character into our social existence, we might be able to contribute to the collective world without losing our critical distance from this world. Equally important, we might get a chance to give birth to new versions of ourselves without thereby completely losing touch with the old ones.

6

Existential tangles such as these can feel intimidating. And what makes things even trickier is that there is no general method that works for everyone. Only trial and error can teach us how to combine our character with our social investments, which is why so many of us give up. Yet giving up can be imprudent, for it only ensures that when the voice of our character finally ruptures our defenses, it does so with a fury that topples the major pillars of our existence. Furthermore, trading in our character makes us prey to the deep nihilism of our society. I have already pointed out that this nihilism implies that what we believe makes little difference—that having strong passions, strong aspirations, is not only futile, but also a little embarrassing. Add to this the political inertia of thinking that our actions bear no weight, that no matter what we do, those who wield power run the world more or less as they please, and it becomes clear why many of us feel that regardless of how hard we try, we cannot make a dent in the world's hardened surface.

There are of course those who would say that it is pointless to worry about any of this—that the world in which we live punishes those who care too much. And there are also those who would say that our social environment makes a mockery of notions such as character and the truthfulness of desire. This environment is made up of images, facades, pretenses, and performances. There is a drastic shallowness to it, so that how we look or act is more important than how we, in the privacy of our being, feel. To get ahead, all we need to do is to play our part with panache and sometimes even a bit of daring flamboyance. In point of fact, the role we choose to play eventually becomes who we "are": our unique character is nothing but a manifestation of the various disguises we have worn over the years. It is useless, then, to agonize about having misplaced our authentic character, for "authenticity" is merely a matter of effectively internalizing the role we have adopted.

This way of looking at things has some validity, for obviously who we are, at any given point in time, is always in some sense the culmination of what we have done. We learn to be socially viable human beings by internalizing a set of performative codes that tell us how to act. Over time, such codes congeal into a semicoherent identity; they solidify into an awareness of self that feels so utterly compelling to us that we cannot even imagine being someone else. Indeed, we tend to possess a fairly ritualized repertoire of regular performances—performances that have become so deep seated, so thoroughly "us," that they have crystallized into an affective configuration that appears more or less immutable. In this sense, it is true that we all learn to be specific kinds of people through specific kinds of performances we repeat throughout our lives.[3] But this does not change the fact that some performances seem to communicate something about the authenticity of our character, whereas others fall short of it; it does not banish our sense that some of our self-performances come closer to capturing the distinctive inflection of our desire than others.

The matter is complicated by the fact that even the most entrenched performative repertoire remains an open system where new layers of self-fashioning are constantly being introduced at the same time as old ones are falling into the background. Some of these new layers do not in any way shake our self-conception because they align so neatly with our understanding of who we are that adding them to our repertoire feels as uncomplicated as adding a piece to a puzzle. But when a new layer arrives in the guise of the kind of event I have described, there is immediately a discrepancy between our stockpile of regular performances and the new life direction we are invited to pursue. In such cases, the new direction feels so engaging that we start to intuit that our usual performances have somehow led us astray. And when we catch ourselves sliding back and unwittingly repeating a performance from our old repertoire, we feel as if we were short-changing some higher potential of ours. Our sense of desolation arises from a disparity between who we have grown into as a result of our customary way of living and the new ideal, the new rendering of ourselves, that we are reaching for. This is why there is no contradiction between the performative nature of our identities and our yearning for authenticity: no matter how "constructed" our self, there is a specificity to our ideals that allows us to distinguish between satisfying and unsatisfying existential itineraries. In effect, the realization that our self is created through performative choices only increases our capacity to steer it into the desired direction because it by definition opens up the possibility of new kinds of existential possibilities (after all, what has been constructed can usually be reconstructed). And if we repeatedly make choices that correspond to our ideals, we increase our chances of fashioning the kind of life that feels worth living.

7

All of this of course presupposes that we have ideals to begin with—and that we are capable of forging new ones. The reason nihilism is so problematic is that implies that our current world is the only possible world, that the way things are in our lives, or in society at large, is how they will always be. In other words, when we cease to be driven by our passions, when our aspirations no longer have the power to incite us, we become incapable of conceiving alternatives to our reality. The effect is in fact very much like the effect of being caught up in the repetition compulsion: we cannot even begin to envision new modes of organizing our lives; we shrink the space of creativity so that new ideals, values, goals, and ambitions cannot enter the world.

Recent advances in how we understand knowledge production—in particular the realization that our inherited beliefs are not immutable facts, truths, or certainties, but rather the result of centuries of human efforts to figure out how the world works—have ironically made it easier to fall into a fully relativistic worldview where the distinction between right and wrong, noble and corrupt, is dim at best. I would never want to trade away these advances, for they have opened a space for the kinds of meanings that were foreclosed by more traditional worldviews, thereby offering a chance for previously suppressed voices and outlooks to enter into the collective process of meaning production. But there is no doubt that they have also made it easier not to care, for if we believe that the world is filled with mere "opinions," mere individual perspectives, then it becomes difficult to justify feeling very strongly about any particular way of thinking. Additionally, the realization that there may be no definitive "point" to our lives—such as religious redemption or transcendent metaphysical insight—can induce us to see the world's offerings as hollow and insincere.[4] Nihilism of this kind reflects our awareness that although there are countless sites of interest that surround us, few of them can arouse our commitment in any substantial fashion. It causes us to denounce all hopes for a better future as too utopian. And it drives us into the folds of the kind of pragmatism that tells us that the only thing that matters is the nitty-gritty of our daily lives, and particularly our material success, so that making money becomes the only aspiration that still has the power to stir us.

This pragmatism is of course not merely a personal failing, but a problem that results in part from the overly utilitarian, overly results-oriented organization of our late capitalist consumer society. This society functions by homogenizing desires, by leveling distinctions between people, so as to better sell its products. In a way, the deluge of different commodities available to us merely conceals the degree to which our desires are being reconditioned to want what the market can provide; the fact that we have so many options available to us does not mean that our desires are variable, but merely that we are being taught to desire a spectrum of things within the globalized structure of our economy—a structure that advances a very specific vision of what is desirable. Furthermore, this economy is compelling us to work inhumanly long hours, in some cases because doing so is the only way to survive, in others because it is the only way to be successful in one's profession. Working-class people often hold several jobs because they cannot make ends meet with just one; white-collar employees often work around the clock because this is what is expected of them in high-pressure professional environments, such as law firms, universities, and investment companies. The outcome is that no one has time to pause for long enough to linger in thought, let alone devise new ideals. One way in which our current system keeps us docile, both personally and politically, is by depriving us of the necessary mental space to conceive of alternative means of organizing our lives. If it is so adept at generating nihilism, it is because it is so good at crushing our imaginations.

The singular code of ethics introduced by the event—like the singular code of ethics introduced by the Thing's echo—counters such nihilism because it compels us to utter a rebellious "no" whenever we are asked to betray the truth of our desire (or character). In the same way that the Thing's echo makes mundane objects reverberate with an exceptional dignity, thereby fending off the complacency that divests the world of higher aspirations, the event introduces a current of passion into our everyday lives. By reminding us that what we believe does makes a difference, it reopens the possibility of new possibilities, allowing us to bring new ideals, values, goals, and ambitions into the world. What is more, it invites us to take an active interest in something larger than ourselves. This is the case with those who get invested in political struggles as well as with those who devote their lives to helping others, be it as humanitarians, activists, or other service providers. And it is also the case with those who give their lives over to science and the advancement of knowledge. Even artists and inventors who "lose" themselves in their projects can be said to become a part of something more urgent than their personal concerns in the sense that their creations will over time become a constituent of the social fabric we all share. Their passions, in ushering them "beyond" their daily preoccupations, also usher them "beyond" their own lives in ways that benefit all of us. This is one reason that actualizing the self is sometimes the same thing as surrendering it, allowing it (momentarily at least) to dissolve into a greater cause in the same way that a raindrop dissolves into the ocean.

8

The Upside of Anxiety

The admonitions to be happy . . . have about them the fury of
the father berating his children for not rushing joyously down-
stairs when he comes home irritable from his office.

—Theodor Adorno

1

In his incisive critique of Western bourgeois society, Theodor
Adorno notes the hegemonic nature of the cultural injunction to
be happy, arguing that if we are constantly assailed by the idea
that we should lead cheerful, pleasure-filled lives, it is because our
participation in this creed makes us easier to manipulate. It dis-
tracts us from the collective ills of our society—such as poverty
and inequality—by inducing us to direct our attention to the coordinates of our own comfort. It makes us politically acquiescent by
causing us to locate the source of our happiness within our own
being, so that we no longer recognize that some of our unhappiness might be socially generated; it shifts the responsibility for
happiness from society to the self, making it less likely that we
will agitate for social change.[1] Along related lines, this injunction

generates an ever more privatized, more circumscribed notion of what happiness means in the first place, with the result that we deem ourselves happy when we are leading relatively trouble-free, relatively stable lives focused on the minutia of our personal interests. And nothing, Adorno claims, feeds this state of affairs more than the archetype of a genuine, authentic life propagated by our culture—an archetype that tells us that our lives have no meaning unless we are able to give voice to the deep spontaneity of our being. This ideology raises authenticity to a fetish, leading Adorno to remark, with his characteristic peevishness, that anything that does not wish to wither should "take on itself the stigma of the inauthentic."[2]

On the surface, it may seem that the cultivation of character I have been discussing in this book might participate in the bourgeois dream of genuine, authentic lives that Adorno so despises. But I hope to have shown that something more complicated is at stake. Indeed, I think that my project actually shares important connections with that of Adorno, for as much as he ridicules the bourgeois mentality that, in the name of authenticity, decries the decay of the individual and the loss of our spiritual substance, he is simultaneously deeply suspicious of the ways in which our socioeconomic organization, along with the culture industry that both reflects and supports this organization, objectifies and alienates us, deadening our faculties in the manner that Marx already analyzed.[3] Moreover, as I noted at the beginning of this book, I am not envisioning the authenticity of character as some sort of an essential core of being that it is our duty to bring into expression. And I am definitely not aligning it with the simplistic over-the-counter portrayals of well-adjusted lives that circulate in our culture. Quite the contrary, the argument I have been developing implies that the more prominence we give to our character, the more existential upheaval, and therefore the more maladjustment, we might need to be able to tolerate. If it is true, as I have been proposing, that our character expresses something about the most rebellious and socially resistant echelons of our being, then being summoned by it is not necessarily a comfortable experience; and, as we saw in the previous chapter, it is rarely a purely individual-istic endeavor, but rather one that connects us to a cause larger than ourselves.

To state the matter with some austerity, the price of extend-ing an invitation to the least-regimented aspects of our identity is anxiety and its close cousin: overagitation. In this context, it is important to remember that anxiety is not just a matter of being vulnerable to the various assaults of the world, but in many ways intrinsic to our constitution. Our bodies are easily overstimulated. And our psyches can get so overexcited that we lose control of our thought processes and emotions. Generally speaking, there is a kind of relentless unruliness to human life that arises from within ourselves and that forces us to live in a constant state of potential breakdown. We are always in danger of losing our balance, so that stretches of serenity may well be the exception, whereas a degree of anxiety is the normal state of life. Although some people are certainly more prone to it than others, and although most of us are more prone to it in some situations than in others, we cannot usually rid ourselves of it completely. Yet we are under constant social pressure to do so.

2

It may help to think about the conflict between the relative orderli-ness of our social existence and the potentially disorderly (anxi-ety-inducing) nature of our character as follows. The formative processes of socialization that gradually draw us into the composi-tion of collective life organize our world on ever-increasing levels of sophistication. In the same way that we cannot learn calculus before we have learned that two plus two equals four, our ability to tackle life on more complex levels grows progressively. By the time we are adults, we have come to master a huge number of skills that lend consistency to our lives. We know that if we do X, Y will fol-low: we place the right ingredients in a pot, and soup will follow; we practice the piano diligently, and our playing improves; we pay our bills on time, and our credit rating goes up; we work assiduously, and we get promoted; we raise our children wisely, and they grow into well-behaved adults. Of course, there are times when things do not quite work out this way, when we burn the soup, get laid off rather than promoted, or watch our children turn into self-satisfied, arrogant tyrants. But, in principle, we learn that there is a correlation between certain kinds of actions and certain kinds of outcomes.

In contrast, when we are called to our character, this correlation no longer holds. This is because our character elicits the participation of layers of our being that are more elemental than our social identity, including bodily energies that have been organized only in the most rudimentary manner conceivable. These elemental layers are of course not the only thing our character is made of. And, as I have explained, even they have not fully escaped the imprint of the social. Nevertheless, in the same way that ideals that correspond to the truth of our desire preserve some distance from culturally dominant ideals, our character cannot be conflated with the polite and more or less compliant front we stage for the consumption of others. Its makeup includes largely asocial (or minimally social) energies that can defeat the disciplined contours of our social persona, which is why I have stressed that it almost inevitably represents the disobedient underside of our culturally intelligible identity. I have, in effect, started to suggest that, unfortunately for us, the energies that rescue us from an excessive loyalty to anesthetizing social formations are also the ones that, time and again, throw us out of kilter with the notion of a sensible life. This is why it would be difficult to conjure away anxiety without conjuring away what is most defiant about us; it would be difficult to free us of anxiety without making us a little submissive.

This difficulty should make us more than a little skeptical of the fact that tranquility and peace of mind are such sought-after commodities in our society. Granted, it is nice to feel calm. Granted, there is nothing wrong with a bit of serenity. Many of us could probably benefit from some meditation and mindfulness. But, as I have remarked, there can be an obsessiveness to the pursuit of tranquility that implies that the good life consists of banishing all tension from our universe. From magazine articles that offer us tips on overcoming stress to New Age gurus who equate enlightenment with the ability to fend off agitation, we are inundated by the idea that there is something wrong with us when we allow anxiety to infiltrate our lives. Yet it is quite possible that the more we pursue "balance," the more socially disengaged, the more bland and boring, we become; it is conceivable that the more we buy into the ideal of existential harmony, the more we curb our character.

This may be one reason that Adorno asserts that there is nothing as normalizing as our society's fixation on the notion that we should attain perfect health of both body and mind. Not only are we expected to be exuberantly happy, but we are expected to be devoid of all pathology. And if we cannot quite succeed—if we must exhibit some signs of ill-being—then at least our symptoms should be easily classifiable. That is, even our diseases should fall under the rubric of this or that socially intelligible malfunction, this or that documented disease, which is why Adorno believes that underneath our quest for vibrant health lurks a tragic kind of discreet death: the demise of everything that is eccentric and messy about human life.[4] According to this account, what the socioeconomic system cannot tolerate is a symptom that cannot be locked into a taxonomy, for a lack of taxonomy implies the impossibility of treatment, and treatment is what, above all, must be ministered, lest the system lose its army of well-functioning workers who ensure its smooth operation. If you get a cold, take some decongestants; if you get depressed, take some antidepressants; and if you get anxious, take some sedatives—the important thing is that you make it to your desk on time every morning.

Tim Dean has made a related argument about our society's unparalleled (and historically specific) enthusiasm for the idea that illness can be kept at bay through the meticulous management of our bodies: the avoidance of risk factors such as smoking, drinking, and sexual promiscuity as well as the promotion of a balanced diet and regular exercise are supposed to guarantee our longevity.[5] To a degree, this is obviously true, but it is also a way to moralize illness, to cast judgment on those who fail to adhere to the right regimen. Ultimately, what we are dealing with is a regulation of pleasure—a process of medicalization that tells us which kinds of pleasures are acceptable and which are not.[6] In addition, because of advances in medical diagnostics, we are constantly being screened for future illnesses, so that even when we are perfectly healthy, we are living in an atmosphere of doom where, at any given moment, something *might* go wrong. The smallest nodule that shows up on a CT scan will be tracked for the rest of our lives unless we put a stop to this ritual by refusing the annual dose of radiation it requires. Health, in other words, has been recast as a precarious state that needs constant monitoring, assessment, and surveillance. As a consequence, we often spend more energy on fretting about potential problems than we do on fixing already existing ones, scrutinizing our bodies with the kind of watchfulness that borders on paranoia. And, maddeningly, all of this is happening at the same time as many people are denied access to basic health care.

I am not saying that we should give up all attempts to adhere to a healthy lifestyle or that medical screening should be suspended. Both can obviously have huge benefits. But there is something rather dismal about the fact that so many of us forget to feel alive because we are constantly worried about being (prematurely) dead. And I agree with Dean that there is a link between the interminable exercise in health management that many of us succumb to without complaint and the more general preoccupation with risk that is the hallmark of contemporary culture. The rhetoric of risk that surrounds topics such as national security and terrorism, for instance, can make us excessively apprehensive so that the rhetoric itself becomes a (less acute but nevertheless insidious) form of terrorization. And, sadly, this rhetoric can render us fearful of everything that seems unfamiliar to us, such as different races, religions, or nationalities.[7] Yet the idea that we can somehow expunge all risk from our lives is as unrealistic as the idea that we might live forever. In point of fact, I suspect that beneath our society's desperate attempts to minimize risk—and to prescribe happiness—there lurks a wretched impotence in the face of the intrinsically insecure nature of human existence. As a society, we have arguably lost the capacity to cope with this insecurity in the sense that we do not know how to welcome it into the current of our lives. Instead, we do everything we can to deny it through pragmatic measures that give us an illusion of control at the same time as they dampen our ability to address the core of the matter—namely, the question of how we might be able to admit risk into our lives without giving it undue power.

3

There are clearly different varieties of risk: some can be counteracted more effectively than others. But it is helpful to keep in mind that the minute we desire, we bring risk into our lives, for desire, as I have demonstrated, connects us to an outside world that is always inherently unpredictable. How each of us carves a viable foothold within this reality is far from self-evident. Where we invest our energies, how we respond to the challenges of life, where we discern an opening (as opposed to a closed door), and how we come to have the courage to step through that opening are conundrums that do not have simple solutions. Consequently, if there is a "point" to our existential struggles, it is not to help us internalize the clear-cut answers on offer in our society, but rather to teach us to perceive the deceptive nature of such answers. If there is a "meaning" to life, it is that there is no definitive meaning, but merely our recurring efforts to arrive at forms of meaning that are somehow meaningful to us specifically. On this view, what is meaningful to me may not be so to you, but what we share is that both of us are engaged in our own unique quest for something that will make our lives feel worthwhile. In addition, the contours of this quest tend to shift over time so that what we find compelling at a particular moment may not be so later. This is fortunate, for if the meaning of our lives were not reset from time to time, the stream of life would quickly outrun us, so that we would be "out of date" with our own lives; we would find ourselves out of step with the forward-moving cadence of our existence. The fact that the meaning of our lives evolves with the rest of our concerns ensures that this meaning remains meaningful; it ensures that there is a connection between our lived reality and the meaning we attribute to this reality.

Unquestionably, there are times when we fall behind. There are times when we lose track of the meaning of our existence because the stream of our lives moves so swiftly that we cannot quite keep up. One day, we look up and wonder how we ended up where we are. And we may realize that where we are is not necessarily where we want to be. These times are often moments of existential crisis—moments when we are forced to slow down and perhaps even to settle into our anxiety (or sadness or disenchantment) in order to take a more careful look at where we are headed. During such moments, it may feel that we are wasting enormous amounts of time. But they may in fact be some of the most productive points of our lives, for they tend to produce insights that we could not arrive at if our lives kept up their usual fast tempo. Moreover, whenever we find it impossible to do what we are used to doing, we may be able to do something different—something that in the long run proves to be more consequential than our present activity. In this sense, being arrested by a crisis of some sort can have constructive consequences: it can prompt us to modify the track we are on so that meaning once again becomes available to us.

During moments of crisis, when we feel that our time is running out, it is easy to get distressed about the ephemeral nature of life. But even this is not always a bad thing. Much of the time, we suppress the awareness that our lives will not endure. If we did not, we might not be able fend off desolation. When you stop to think about it, it is a minor miracle that most of us find a way to get out of bed in the morning, for the recognition that our lives are destined to end is a formidable burden to carry around. We understandably do not like to think about it. Yet consistently ignoring the issue can cause us to squander a lot of life; it can cause us to live carelessly so that we end up doing many things that ultimately do not matter to us. The so-called midlife crisis may be nothing more than the realization that time is about to run out and that we must consequently do things that matter. The trouble is that by the time this happens, we often do not have the foggiest idea of what matters, so that we are driven to look for the meaning of our lives in all the wrong places. From this perspective, being thrown into an existential crisis that forces us to think about the brevity of life might be an auspicious event even if we, at the time, find it difficult to read it as such. People who have endured a number of such crises may be more troubled. Their overall character may be a shade sadder. But they may have a better idea of what they want out of the rest of their lives. And, as a result, they may be better able to pursue the right kinds of aspirations.

Somewhat paradoxically, remaining cognizant of the fleeting character of life may allow us to fully appreciate the enormity of the gift we have been given. In the best of circumstances, we might be able to stop mourning life's bitter brevity and come, instead, to see this brevity as the melancholy lining of its preciousness. If we thought that we were going to live forever, we would be unlikely to approach our days with any degree of passion; we would not know how to treasure any of the moments the make up those days. My earlier account of how our sense of lack causes us to devise various strategies for compensating for it is relevant here, for in the same way that our awareness that something is missing from our lives generates renewed feats of creativity, our recognition that there is an end to our lives gives rise to renewed efforts to fill the time we have left with objects and activities that we experience as satisfying. This is exactly how we arrive at higher ideals, higher aspirations. One might even say that although complacency is common, it is deeply antithetical to human life because our consciousness of life's impending end forces us to care. In a way, it is the prospect of death rather than life itself that compels us to reach for more life.[8] As a consequence, life's transience does not diminish its value but rather augments it, so that to love our fate means, among other things, to love the evanescence of life.[9]

4

An important part of coping with life's evanescence is being able to release earlier versions of the self. I have argued that we are historical creatures who have a consciousness of self in part because we have a consciousness of our personal history; even though components of this history remain obscure, we do have a memory of many of the things that have gone into our constitution. At the same time, our process of becoming ensures that no particular incarnation of the self is the final one. As a result, one of the challenges of life is to learn to relinquish old incarnations of ourselves whenever new ones are gathering momentum. This relinquishment can be difficult, particularly if we happen to like the old incarnation. It can, for example, be hard to let go of a younger version of ourselves because that version seemed to have more energy, freedom, or attractiveness than the new version. In other words, if it is sometimes hard to discard the past because the pain of this past haunts our present, it can also be hard to give up a past that has been particularly rewarding; it can be hard to surrender what has brought a great deal of satisfaction. Yet if we are to give fresh editions of ourselves a chance, we must find a way of doing so.

Life asks us to mourn each passing incarnation of the self. This amounts to a lifetime of mourning. There will always be regrets and misgivings. We tend to get nostalgic about parts of our past that made us happy. And we tend to grieve the loss of certain opportunities: we lament having made this choice rather than that, of having taken this turn rather than that. But most of all, we mourn those aspects of ourselves that we are forced to renounce because they have become redundant. Sometimes our mourning is so intense that we cannot bring it to a timely conclusion but instead form melancholy attachments to dimensions of ourselves that are largely obsolete. Yet relying on an out-of-date version of ourselves is equivalent to pouring milk that has gone bad into our coffee. It sours our existence, sometimes even making us sick. This is why learning to mourn and gently dispose of old versions of the self is essential for our continued ability to feel that our lives have meaning.

Shedding earlier incarnations of the self is a precondition of staying existentially alert. More specifically, the creative crafting of a life pays attention to how the past, present, and future interact with each other. It does not shun the past, for it knows that the past is the source of current strength, not to mention character. But it also looks to the future because it knows that the future holds the promise of unrealized potential. Even though the future always contains a more or less audible echo of the past, and even though it is sometimes genuinely frightening, it is also often teeming with new opportunities, with new modalities of life (and love). As such, it is at once a place of desire and an opening to hope—an invitation to actively participate in the fashioning of our lives. But doing so requires the willingness to transcend the self that worships the past as the bedrock of its existence; it requires the willingness to take risks and to tolerate the anxiety that comes with these risks, for it is only by welcoming the unknown that we can outgrow the known. Most important, as I have suggested at various points in this book, accepting the invitation of the future entails the readiness to undertake the somewhat mysterious alchemy of translating the wisdom of the past into a resource for living in the future; it entails the capacity to learn from the past without becoming unnecessarily faithful to the forms of life that belong to this past. I have emphasized that it would be a tremendous waste to bury the wisdom we have garnered from the past. Yet it would also be a waste to stay so wedded to it that we are incapable of striding into the future. This is exactly why there is nothing that adds to our existential agility more than the ability to use the various elements of the past—the good and the bad alike—as ingredients of the future.

5

I have stressed that a vital component of being able to use the past as a resource for the future is the capacity to translate bad things into good—or at least better—things. We all are familiar with the myth of the Phoenix rising from the ashes. There is a reason this myth is so central to our cultural imagination, for the capacity to bounce back from failure, to reemerge from the rubble of hardship, destruction, disappointment, or emotional (and sometimes even physical) devastation, is an important value in our society. It may well be that the rhetoric of turning adversity into opportunity on some level panders to the interests of our acutely competitive capitalist society—a society that, implicitly at least, upholds "survival of the fittest" as a principle of conduct. And there is no doubt that the buoyant advice on how to conquer hardship that you might find in your average self-help guide, lifestyle magazine, or Hollywood movie is just as banal as the injunction to be happy that Adorno criticizes. The cult of the hero who triumphs against all odds may be an essential part of American folklore, yet there are times when it is entirely hollow. And there are even times when it is offensive, for it clearly is not the case that all privation, all suffering or sadness, can be overcome. The privation that originates from social inequality can ravage a person without delivering him or her to the threshold of any new opportunity. The suffering caused by terminal illness (or some other personal tragedy) can be hard to transmute into hopefulness. And the sadness of losing someone irreplaceable can be impossible to eliminate, at least for a very long time.

My evocation of the image of the Phoenix rising is therefore not an attempt to deny the heartbreaking (or soul-pulverizing) realities of pain. My point is merely that *some* varieties of pain are amenable to being converted into existential acumen, and even distilled into character, and that the image of the Phoenix reflects this possibility. It expresses something about our awareness that we need a degree of hardship to grow, that obstacles and impediments are, in a broadly existential sense, crucial for our development. Even if on one level we tend to think that the more difficult our lives, the less successful they are, on another we understand that difficulties are often necessary for self-renewal—that sometimes our failures are more productive than our successes. In the same way that giving up an earlier version of the self makes room for a new version, what seems like a failure may make room for the kinds of successes that we might not have been able to attain without this failure. For example, the disappointment of a desire can become a source of a new desire—one that will eventually lead to something even more satisfying than what the original desire could ever have delivered.

Failures are gateways to new opportunities. They are often (by no means always, but often) life's roundabout way of getting us to our destination. Although we would prefer to live without them, they can be effective in spurring us to new personal plot lines whenever our habitual ones have ceased to function properly. Take an extreme scenario: a breakdown that tears the fabric of our lives so badly that we become despondent. No matter how painful such a breakdown is, in the long run it can yield to a different kind of life—one that allows us to access previously unexplored territories of personal meaning. Although there is certainly always the possibility that a breakdown is just a breakdown, giving us nothing in return, it can also, precisely because it destroys the customary structure of our lives, become an occasion for existential configurations that are not tenable within that structure. And inasmuch as it allows whatever has been sidelined in our being to finally speak its passion, it can serve as a portal to something genuinely enlivening, provided we give it enough time to mature into insight.

We can never know ahead of time which of our experiences will eventually become meaningful to us. Sometimes it takes decades for the significance of a given event to unfurl. We may be seventy-five before we realize that some spirit-crushing failure actually gave us a valuable resource, such as strength, resilience, humility, or the capacity to hear other people's pain. This is why I believe that the most "successful" lives are frequently ones that are also the most acquainted with failure. If nothing else, this outlook might allow us to stop trying to force our lives into specific outcomes. After all, if we cannot know which of our experiences will in the end lead to something worthwhile and which will not, there is no advantage to limiting ourselves to ones that on the surface appear victorious. I do not mean that we should not readjust our course when it is clearly not taking us where we want to go. But there is a difference between attempting to live with a degree of discernment and discrimination, on the one hand, and attempting to control what is beyond our control, on the other. There are things in the present, as there were things in the past, that happen without our being able to do anything to stop them. Recognizing this is not of matter of fatalism, but of learning to live in a less compulsive manner.

6

If the only thing that is certain about life is its uncertainty, our best course of action might be to step into its moments of failure, and even of breakdown, with the expectation that something of worth might eventually come out of them. Furthermore, given that our character rarely speaks in measured terms—that the distinction between being called to our character and being overagitated is difficult to uphold—it may be unrealistic to think that we can have a character without anxiety. Because the breaking through of character is often accompanied by a breaking through of excess energy, the art of living a singular life may lead to thoroughly awkward, anxiety-ridden displays of surplus ardor and devotion. This is one reason that the search for existential harmony prescribed by our culture can be so profoundly misguided. If what is most singular about us is linked to what is most volatile about our being, then the attempt to achieve composure can only rob us of distinctiveness. I am by no means saying that we should actively court instability or that composure has no place in our lives. Much of the time, we cannot survive without a measure of poise and self-possession. Yet the account of character I have been advancing compels us to admit that what really counts in life is not our ability to evade chaos, but rather our capacity to meet it in such a way as to not be irrevocably broken. We need to be able to transform the wayward energies of our character into a livable actuality—one that honors our singularity without at the same time making it untenable for us to participate in collective systems of sociality as well as in more intimate networks of relationality.

The quest for equilibrium might therefore not always be all that it's cracked up to be. And I would be equally suspicious of another darling idea of our culture, namely that greater degrees of inner integration lead to greater degrees of well-being. To some extent, this is indeed the case. But, as I have tried to illustrate, there can be something quite ruthless about the attempt to impose an artificial sheen of stability on an inherently unstable psychological and emotional reality. In extreme cases, it can lead to a stiffness of deportment that makes it impossible for us to embrace the more erratic expressions of our character. This is why those who have ordered their lives too tightly—who have constructed a bastion of regularizing routines against the specter of anxiety—often have trouble deciphering the truth of their desire, with the consequence that although their lives may be well managed, they are also a little anemic.

As much as we might fear the destabilizing energies of our character, we also profit from their relentless pulse in the sense that this pulse repeatedly replenishes us. If this were not the case, we would quickly begin to stagnate. That is, it is precisely because our social persona is not entirely impervious to the rebellious energies of our character that we are capable of renewing ourselves on a regular basis. From this perspective, self-cultivation entails a dynamic interplay between the disciplined and undisciplined layers of our being. Though we need the orderliness of the former for socially practicable lives, we also need the disorderliness of the latter as a countermeasure to existential sterility. This is why fleeing from our constitutive agitation, and particularly from our tendency toward anxiety, may be a mistake, for this agitation can serve as a catalyst for the revival of tired or otherwise floundering modalities of living.

7

The notion of agitation as catalyst should not be confused with the idea that there is nothing to be done with the excesses of anxiety. I am not saying that we have to resign ourselves to its most symptomatic manifestations. In this context, it is useful to recall that a symptom is at bottom a method of binding energy that has no other place to go. This implies that to the extent that we are able to devise an effective way of discharging our excess energy, we might be able to dodge the most voracious of symptoms. Many high-achieving individuals, for instance, are successful in part because they have found a suitable outlet for the surplus of energy that courses through their bodies and minds. Consciously or unconsciously, such individuals understand that they have a choice between pathology and achievement, that the less they are able to pour their tension into their accomplishments, the more likely it is to erupt in painful symptoms, obsessions, neuroses, and addictions of various kinds. This may seem like a sad state of affairs, and it may also be an addiction of sorts, but it is argu-ably one of the least destructive means of processing anxiety. This is why I have always been slightly suspicious of therapists who tell their patients to "take things easy." There are individuals for whom this piece of advice is just about the worst conceivable, for when you take away their drive to accomplish things, you open the door to a host of alternatives that, all things considered, are much more damaging. There are definitely worse coping mechanisms than achievement.

The trick, once again, is to channel our energies into something the reflects the truth of our desire. This is why Freud proposed that falling in love is a good way to keep ourselves from falling (psychically) ill. It is possible to take this idea literally, for there is undeniably little that binds (and therefore consumes) our energies more successfully than romantic love: there is something about the passionate dedication of love that offers a powerful "cure" to the predicament of not knowing where to invest our energies. But we can also understand Freud's statement more metaphorically, as an indication that we all need anchors for our desire. Some of these anchors are concrete, such as professional aims or creative endeav-ors, but others are wholly intangible, such as higher ideals and aspirations. My point is that, in the absence of such anchors, our surplus energies are likely to flow into symptomatic enactments.

Take spiritual practices. Indeed, take the kinds of practices that, according to our New Age gurus, liberate us from our ego-bound desires. I would propose that their effectiveness is not due to the fact that they free us of desire but, quite the contrary, to the fact that they provide an extraordinarily strong anchor for this desire (ego bound or not): if they "work," it is because they are an efficient means of cathecting energy (including desire), of becoming so single-mindedly focused on a specific objective that everything else falls into the background. They are merely one technique among others for harnessing energy, which, in turn, implies that underneath their calm surface throbs the mutinous pulse of anxiety. The same is true of our other anchors, which is why my problem with popular spirituality is not so much that it tries to surmount anxiety, but that it tends to overstate its chances of success. Our other techniques tend to be more honest in that they admit partial defeat. Even when they curtail our restlessness, they tend to acknowledge its continued presence, so that it makes no sense to talk about love without agitation, professional aims or creative endeavors without trepidation, or higher ideals and aspirations without apprehension.

When we use our various anchors deftly (rather than dogmatically), we do not deny anxiety. Though we seek to contain it through our activity so as to keep it from overpowering us, we remain aware of it as the potentially explosive background of our pursuits. Most important, we welcome the portion of it that seeps through our defenses as a sign of our singularity. Adorno states that an awkward, embarrassing gesture can preserve "a trace of vanished life."[10] Hannah Arendt in turn talks about an ethereal aura that is implicit in our gestures, in our speech and actions, but that cannot be reduced to our qualities (our talents, limitations, and so on). This inimitable aura tells others "who" we are rather than "what" we are, and it can be subdued only in complete silence or inaction. Like the Greek daimon, which was thought to represent an individual's unique identity and was believed to accompany him or her throughout life, our aura is easily visible to others yet impossible to translate into a clear description.[11] I like to think of Arendt's daimon and Adorno's awkward, embarrassing gesture together because I believe that their intersection is where we find the entity that I have been depicting as our character. Like the daimon, this character is intangible yet irrepressible. And like the awkward, embarrassing gesture, it communicates something about the often quite excessive (unreasonable, immoderate) compilation of energy that infuses our lives with vitality. Anxiety represents one facet of this energy, which is why it is not always the enemy that our society makes it out to be. Quite often, it is merely what reminds us of what it means to want what we may have forgotten to want.

9

The Erotics of Being

The day is a space for the potential articulation of my idiom.
—Christopher Bollas

1

Being able to integrate anxiety into our art of living is an important part of crafting a character. But, ultimately, we need more; we need to be able not just to cope with volatility, but also to experience joy. This is why I appreciate Christopher Bollas's description of the day as a space for the articulation of our "idiom."[1] According to this vision, each day offers us a choice: either we can approach it in a way that expresses something of our character, or we can fail to do so by flooding it with character-suppressing objects and activities. As I have been arguing, there are objects and activities that release our idiosyncratic spirit, helping us actualize ourselves on a more complex level. And there are others that do not do a whole lot for us but rather waste our resources by guiding us to banal preoccupations. The latter are often purely habitual.

When we let our habits become too rigid, we no longer have a good sense of how to turn the day into a rewarding space; we no longer know how to select vitalizing objects and activities, with the result that we squander the day's promise. If each day begins with potentialities that we can either honor or betray, nothing is easier than betraying these potentialities. If it is tempting to betray the "event" in Badiou's sense, it may be even more tempting to betray each and every day. In fact, many of us do so on a regular basis without realizing that this is what we are doing. And then we complain that the day "got away" from us.

There are of course times when letting the day "get away" is the right thing to do—when doing nothing in particular or doing something that we did not intend to do is the best articulation of our character. Some of the most delectable things in life arise when we allow the day (or even the week) to slip away without worrying too much about what we might lose in the process. In addition, much of the time we have little choice about how we spend our days. Many of us are obliged to do the kind of work that we do not particularly enjoy because it is the only way to keep ourselves financially afloat. Or we may have to clean the apartment when we would rather be reading a novel. Or some minor crisis may demand attention exactly when we have picked up the thread of some desired activity. I would never want to suggest that all objects and activities are available to us and even less that they are available to us in an equal manner. One of the terribly unfair things about the world is that some of us have a great deal of freedom of choice, whereas others are constrained in countless different ways. From this perspective, there can be a deep arrogance to the idea that we should fill our days only with the sorts of objects and activities that somehow inspire us.

However, to the extent that we *do* have a choice, it would be a mistake to turn away from objects and activities that speak to us on a level that resonates with our character; it would be a mistake to blunt their evocative summons. We have already seen that the people we invite into our lives have a tremendous impact on our destinies. But there is also an endless array of inanimate items that populate our world. From books, rooms, cafes, music, and websites to the carrots in our fridge, the soap in our shower, and the clothes in our closet, we interact with things that determine the shape of our day. Bollas emphasizes that not all of these things are created equal, that some objects are better than others in ushering us to the heart of satisfying experience.[2] Similarly, some activities engage us in meaningful ways, whereas others fill us with lassitude. Against this backdrop, what is so sad about life is that many of us routinely (and voluntarily) pour our energies into objects and activities that cannot bring us any real satisfaction.

A great deal, then, depends on our ability to choose the right kinds of objects and activities. When we choose prosaic ones—ones that do not have the power to move us—we cannot accede to a place of everyday wonder. But when we choose well, our character thrives. This is not necessarily a matter of selecting objects and activities that carry social prestige; it is not a matter of going to the theater rather than watching television, or of going to a museum rather than reading a comic book, because we know that, culturally speaking, the former activities are more highly valued than the latter. Rather, it is a matter of choosing those objects and activities that are most characteristically "us"—that bolster the singularity of our being.

It may of course be that we need considerable experience to know which objects and activities best achieve this aim. Perhaps we choose television over theater, and comic books over museums, because we have not had enough exposure to theater and museums to accurately assess their magnificence. Alternatively, perhaps we shun television and comic books because we have not seen the best of what these mediums can offer. Most of us have not had a wide enough range of experiences to make fully informed choices. But many of us can develop a more accurate sense of what stirs us and what does not; by paying closer attention to the choices we make as well as to the feelings that arise from these choices, we can gradually learn to ascertain whether a particular object or activity brings us joy or whether we are reaching for it merely because that is what we are used to doing. To return to the

Lacanian vocabulary I have been using throughout this book, we can learn to distinguish between things that transmit the echo of the Thing and those that do not.

As I have illustrated, we often undertake trivial pursuits (or fill our lives with useless objects that overburden the world) because we fail to recognize the difference between things that contain the Thing's echo and others that merely appear to do so. The latter are simulacra that derail our attention from what really matters. In contrast, when we live according to the truth of our desire, we are more likely to select pursuits that lend vibrancy to our lives. Through our intimate engagement with such pursuits, we acquire the capacity to create a present that, momentarily at least, is compelling enough to elude both the grip of the past and the seductions of the future. Instead of letting the past torment us or the future distract us, we choose to dwell in the present, even if we can do so only for the time being. After all, our process of becoming— our quest to realize more of our potential—would lose much of its significance if we never paused to appreciate the richness of the passing moment. In other words, though the process of becoming is in principle endless, and though, as I have argued, the ability to look toward the future is an essential part of this process, there should also be points along the way when life is "good enough," when it is (and should be) enough to embrace the now even when we know that we are in due course destined to outgrow it. I have already explained why I think that it is a mistake to elevate "the now" into a general philosophy of life, as some New Age approaches do. But at this junction I would like to concentrate on those times when the now is so saturated by meaning and value that we are right to allow ourselves to fall under its spell.

2

What I am getting at amounts to a kind of erotics of being—a mode of experiencing the world that infuses the everyday with a special radiance. In a deeper sense, I am trying to reorient our understanding of the ultimate "purpose" of human life. Many religions teach us that our worldly existence is merely a stepping stone to a more divine realm of redemption. Likewise, many philosophies situate Truth within an otherworldly domain from which we are separated by the diversions of daily experience. From the perspective of these approaches, the culmination of life takes place beyond life: the "transcendent" is what exceeds the world. There is no doubt that such approaches have over the centuries given solace to many people. And they have also propelled countless (and admirable) efforts to solve the mysteries of the universe as well as to touch the sublime through various intellectual, artistic, and spiritual exertions. I have no intention to discredit them in any categorical sense, particularly as I myself have underscored the importance of reaching for what resides beyond our reach (as we do, for instance, when we strive to fill a foundational lack that is inherently unfillable). But I do think that it is worthwhile to reflect on their downside—namely, that as long as we regard transcendence as a matter of escaping the world, it may be difficult for us to appreciate what the world has to offer.

Our religious and philosophical traditions are driven by the impulse to pierce the veil of worldly appearances in order to attain a more transcendent realm of divine grace or metaphysical insight. The trouble with this impulse is that it deprives us of the world by causing us to focus on the otherworldly; it translates our longing for fulfillment—for the lost paradise symbolized by the Thing— into a longing for an otherworldly paradise, thereby diluting our capacity to find substitute satisfactions among the things (objects and activities) of the world. After all, it is hard to linger in our lives when we are interested primarily in what resides beyond them. When we keep thinking that our worldly pursuits are merely a pale reflection of the divine or metaphysical splendor we are after, it is easy to (explicitly or implicitly) denigrate these pursuits; when we reckon that what we can accomplish in the world will never quite measure up, it is easy to downplay the importance of our exertions; and when we fantasize about the end of desire, about an otherworldly place where all desires are at long last satisfied, it is easy to stop trying to satisfy them in the here and now.

Fantasies of otherworldly transcendence thus impoverish the world. They motivate us to chase an otherworldly domain of sublimity so that we become negligent of the ways in which the sublime also resides within the crevices of the world; they make it more difficult for us to remain open to the ways in which the dignity of the Thing resounds in everyday objects and activities. Moreover, pursuing an otherworldly province that promises to deliver us from our worldly suffering can even make us so tolerant of this suffering that we give up our efforts to alleviate it. It can cause us to acquiesce to the idea that suffering—our own or that of others—is a necessary evil to be endured, that it is, quite simply, the price of our salvation. This is what Marx had in mind when he stated that religion is the opiate of the masses: a means of diverting us from suffering by offering us something else to focus on. Although I have myself admitted that pain is an inevitable component of human life, I think that we can sometimes become too used to it. Particularly when we are faced by the suffering of those far away from us, we can all too easily fall back on the conviction that suffering is unavoidable and that there is consequently nothing we can do about it. This is one way in which we arrive at the dubious notion that the inequalities and oppressions of the world are beyond repair—that they are how the world, in some fundamental sense, is meant to be.

3

Ironically, the more we remain enthralled by the dream of transcendence, the less capable we are of attaining its worldly manifestations. This is why I have started to suggest that there are alternatives to the theological and metaphysical accounts of transcendence that have historically dominated our society. Badiou's "event," which, as I have noted, connects us to something larger (more "transcendent") than our private concerns without thereby disparaging the world, is one such alternative. Bollas's conception of the day as a container of potential is another. But these notions are merely two among many ways of conceptualizing what it might mean to be transported "beyond" the routine commonplaces of our lives without having to leave the world behind. The stakes of devising such an unorthodox understanding of transcendence are high, for when we are no longer looking for ways to step out of the rhythm of the everyday, it becomes possible for us to step more fully into this rhythm. In this sense, it is when we stop searching for meaning outside of life that we finally have a real chance of finding it.

When we adjust our aspirations to a level that can actually be attained, we invite "transcendence" into the folds of daily life. This is not to say that our worldly aspirations are always well conceived. Many of us undercut ourselves by the kinds of goals and ambitions that are impossible to achieve. It is as if we replaced the traditional dream of otherworldly salvation with a dream of worldly salvation. Whether we happen to be a woman who cannot eat because she is pursuing the perfect body, a graduate student who cannot write because he is pursuing the perfect dissertation, a father who cannot acknowledge his daughter's accomplishments because he is pursuing the perfect child, or a CEO who cannot take a day off because she is pursuing the perfect company, even our worldly aspirations can keep us from living our lives. In this context, the crafting of character is not a matter of perfecting the self, but rather of perfecting the self's ability to revere its less than perfect incarnations; it is a matter of recognizing that our pursuit of perfection can make us incapable of envisioning a life without it so that we are forever beholden to goals and ambitions that will never materialize. Perfection, after all, is by definition something that belongs to the future—that is always one step ahead of us—so that we are always intrinsically barred from it.

This perception, however, should not be confused with the idea that we should rid ourselves of all ideals, all higher aspirations. As I have sought to demonstrate, we need ideals to fend off an incapacitating nihilism. I am therefore not at all saying that we should reconcile ourselves to our mundane reality without any attempt to improve this reality. I am merely positing that we can improve our reality—that we can carry out inspired acts of reconfiguring this reality—without betraying the world. We can do so because there is a difference between the worldly and the mundane. That is, the world (or the worldly) has plenty of space for things, including ideals, that are not in the least bit mundane. This is exactly why Badiou postulates that there are "immortal" energies within our mortal constitution—that our humble human frames can become vehicles for lofty ideals. And it is also why I have proposed that the best way to resurrect the Thing is to locate its sublime echo within worldly objects and activities. In short, the fact that we cannot rise above the world does not mean that we are irrevocably encased in its most mundane aspects—that we are incapable of anything other than our daily routines.

4

It may help to state the matter as follows: there is a distinction between what is "beyond" the world and what is "other than" the mundane makeup of the world.[3] The fact that we cannot reach "beyond" the world does not mean that we cannot reject its banality—that we cannot aspire toward something "other than" its most commonplace dimensions. One might even say that, in a certain sense, the mundane distances us from the luster of the world just as effectively as do our fantasies of otherworldly transcendence. This is because the mundane is designed to help us survive the world in a pragmatic sense rather than be passionately immersed in it. In other words, although our mundane concerns take place *in* the world, they frequently keep us disconnected from the very world that they seemingly sustain; they distract us from the worldness of the world, as it were. From this viewpoint, being in touch with the pulse of the world is not necessarily the same thing as patiently navigating life's most humdrum affairs. Indeed, it may well be that it is only when we manage (temporarily at least) to disregard our preoccupation with the essentials of existence that we are finally able to see those parts of the world that most merit our admiration—that we become capable of "transcendent" experiences within the confines of our worldly lives.

On this account, we activate the erotics of being whenever we manage to embed ourselves within the details of the world in ways that enable us to bypass the mundane. Among such experiences, of special significance are moments when we devote ourselves to the object or activity in front of us so completely that we either lose track of our surroundings or feel intensely alive within the texture of these surroundings. During such moments, we tend to feel as if we were being seized by an entity greater than ourselves, so that we are no longer the willful agents of our own actions, but rather voluntary captives of some outside force; we become so spellbound by the world's offerings that we momentarily lose track of our usual concerns. Such immediacy of self-experience asks that we allow ourselves to be overtaken by the world so entirely that the normal distinction between self and world becomes permeable. The integrity of both self and world is destabilized, yet this destabilization is also what makes it possible for us to experience the acuteness of both.

Experiences that connect us to the world in this manner— experiences that are worldly without being mundane—can be as simple as breathing in the sharp freshness of October, observing the fog creep up a hillside, letting raindrops tickle our skin, or witnessing how a snowfall muffles a street, making it curiously calm and quiet. Or they can be as complicated as attempting to respond to a friend's barely articulated but palpable distress. There is, in other words, no preordained pattern to what makes us feel mesmerized by the world. We might be captivated by a face, a voice, a landscape, a piece of sculpture, the outlines of a building, an abstract painting, a scientific experiment, a professional goal, or an intimate encounter. We might get swallowed up by a poem, play, movie, or conversation. A summer storm might make us melancholy. A sunny sky might inexplicably oppress our spirits. A newspaper article might shake our convictions. A whiff of perfume might return us to an experience we had forgotten about. The rattle of a broken shutter might recall a childhood confidant. And the way the mountains light up at dawn might make us aware of some potentiality we have neglected. It hardly matters where our attention is directed. What matters is that such experiences tend to grant us an unusual roundedness of being. They make us feel self-actualized in ways that our more mundane activities rarely do. At their most piercing, and particularly at their most disquieting, they rend the fabric of the expected in the same way as Roland Barthes's *punctum*—the mysterious and often quite uncanny detail of a photograph—rends the photographic narrative.[4] And even when they do not arrest us to a spot in this manner, they usually invite us to slow down, so that we can proceed with a greater degree of deliberation than we normally do. When we are particularly lucky, they enable us to discern beauty, value, or merit within something that is seemingly devoid of it.

5

These kinds of transcendent experiences frequently make us feel as if time suddenly stood still. Alternatively, time "flies," so that we are surprised to discover that it is much later than we thought. Either way, we experience an interruption in the ordinary movement of time. We lose track of the passage of time because we are so utterly immersed in what we are doing that we are, so to speak, jolted "outside" of time, dislocated from the usual progression of our lives. The past, present, and future converge into a point of inspired "timelessness." It is as if a little slice of eternity crept into our existence, making it possible for us to invest our entire being in the task (object or activity) at hand. As a matter of fact, such moments tend to engage the body as well as the mind. They entrance us physically as well as mentally because they aim, in a manner of speaking, at something beyond consciousness; they temporarily suspend our rational faculties so as to allow an alternative existential modality to surface. After all, we cannot access what is "other than" the mundane unless we are willing, however fleetingly, to relinquish the (usually fairly rational) underpinnings of the mundane.

Such experiences make us feel as if we were lifted above the mundane. But paradoxically they do so by introducing a kind of self-loss: when we are "lost" in a moment of timelessness, we are also in some ways "lost" to ourselves. Yet such states of self-loss help us find ourselves on a more visceral level. Bollas depicts them as "simple self" experiences—moments of simplified consciousness that enable us to fall into a place "beyond thinking."[5] In a sense, we allow ourselves to be erased so as to come into being in a new way; we let ourselves be transported "beyond" ourselves so as to catch up with ourselves on a more elemental frequency. This type of self-surrender does not diminish us but rather empowers us to experience ourselves, as well as the world, in a more capacious manner. We emerge from it replenished. And because it anchors us in the concrete immediacy of experience, because it allows us to sink into the world rather than (merely) to scrutinize it from a distance, it offers us a kind of temporary release from the burdens of overanalysis: rather than assessing the book we are reading, we simply read; rather than evaluating the conversation we are having, we simply converse; rather than dissecting the erotic encounter we are enjoying, we simply enjoy. We allow ourselves to experience things as they come, without judgment about how they fit into the larger scheme of our lives. At such moments, the larger scheme does not matter. Only the present moment does. And because of this, the moment yields more than it would if we endeavored to control it.

Such states cannot usually be sustained for long. They are by their very nature ephemeral. In the end, we always fall back on the burdens of (over)analysis; we start to worry about the larger scheme of our lives. But even when such transcendent states do not last, they can leave an enduring imprint, a permanent stamp in our psyches that alters the overall tenor of our lives. Understood in this way, they are one means of protecting the integrity of our spirit (or character). They signify a revolt of sorts: a determination to maintain enclaves of singularity that are not fully co-opted by the practical demands of mundane existence. Indeed, they tend to push aside the artificial self-presentations that often mediate our relationship to the collective world so that something more honest can (however transiently) emerge. From this perspective, we value such states not because they are "useful," but because they give us access to more truthful levels of self-experience. To be sure, we may never be able to entirely incorporate such states into our rational universe. Nor can we usually fully capture them in memory. But this does not mean that they do not happen or that they lack reality. They may in fact be the most "real" thing we ever experience.

6

Of particular interest here might be those pursuits where the erotics of being lies dormant within a seemingly mundane activity. Many forms of creativity display such a double valence: a hidden kernel of inspiration that is always in danger of getting lost within the morass of the surrounding banality. Take writing. Those who write for a living know that the popular image of the enraptured writer possessed by the power of the pen is a myth—that there is frequently little about writing that feels transcendent. Writing, like most other varieties of inventiveness, entails long stretches that are fairly boring: the careful collecting and sifting through of materials; the attempt to bring together disparate and at times even antagonistic sources; the act of dismembering conglomerates of ideas so as to detach a piece that is crucial for the endeavor; the endless decisions about what needs to be included and what must be excluded; the somewhat violent process of cutting through the expanse of one's knowledge so as to highlight those elements—and *only* those elements—that advance the argument, intuition, or impression one wishes to communicate; the potentially paralyzing guesswork about how readers might react, what they might accept or reject; the painstaking attempts to build a bridge to minds that do not share one's conceptual universe and that might consequently interpret a given point in a way that it was not intended; the moments of doubt when one loses faith in one's ability to adequately rise to the occasion. And so on.

But then there are those moments of revelation or sudden disclosure when a piece of acumen unexpectedly leaps forth from the muddle of one's materials and stares one in the face with an unremitting boldness. I am referring to those—all too rare—occasions when the various components of the project miraculously click into place to reveal a seedling of insight that one might have sensed all along, but that for one reason or another kept eluding one's grasp. Such epiphanies often appear to arise from some enigmatic (unnamable and rationally inaccessible) depository. It is as if the living tissue of the world opened up to deliver a glistening shard of insight. During such inspired moments, one does not break away from the world. But one does momentarily suspend one's consciousness of its mundane contours. Or, perhaps more accurately, one approaches it from a different plane of consciousness—a plane that feels intensely, almost painfully "real."

I suspect that many creative activities are characterized by a similar vacillation between the mundane and the inspired. And I also suspect that those who are able to manage this vacillation without abandoning the process prematurely are individuals who accept that inspiration does not usually spontaneously descend upon us, but tends to require quite a bit of preparation. The peak experiences that make creativity such a treasured experience flow effortlessly, but they are usually preceded by a great deal of exertion. Although many creative people describe the creative process as one where they feel carried by an uncontrollable force, getting to this point may take a great deal of discipline, practice, and personal sacrifice. Furthermore, it often takes a long time to attain the skills required to translate one's inspiration into a tangible product of some kind; it takes tremendous tenacity to wait for the moment when inspiration meets preparation in just the right way. And it is particularly difficult to keep this combination alive for longer than a brief moment.

This is exactly why Badiou calls attention to the exhaustion or loss of courage that leads artists, scientists, political activists, and sometimes even lovers to betray their calling. Many creative or otherwise inspired pursuits demand the fortitude of persevering even when we feel fatigued, distracted, discouraged, or disillusioned, and even when we momentarily lose sight of the bigger picture (or goal). This kind of fortitude is easier to sustain over time if we recognize that filaments of inspiration tend to be pleated into the substance of the mundane in the same way as deposits of gold are pleated into sediments of rock and sand. The only way to access such filaments is to immerse ourselves within the mundane substance that makes up the bulk of the world (or of the pursuit in question). That is, just as it is usually impossible to find gold without sifting through a mass of baser materials, it is usually impossible to attain the inspired without working through the mire of the mundane. Those creators who are able to convert their visions into concrete artifacts—paintings, sculptures, buildings, novels, poems, melodies, dance routines, mathematical formulas, scientific inventions, and so on—understand this, which is why they do not let their periods of despondency undermine their projects but trust that such periods will in the end open to something that redeems the struggle; they trust that the mundane will, through unremitting effort, deliver the kind of transcendent insight that makes their lives feel worth living.

Another way to explain the issue is to return to the idea that the creative cultivation of character demands the ability to move between relatively organized and relatively disorganized existential states; as I have pointed out, it requires a constant exchange between the social and asocial (or less social) layers of our being. The same principle can be said to apply to our other creative endeavors as well in the sense that they invite us to flirt with self-loss without at the same time giving up our capacity to activate the more regimented requirements of our craft. In other words, creativity entails not only the willingness to regress, to give up structure, but also the ability to reinstate this structure whenever necessary. The fact that this structure often takes the form of prolonged discipline does not cancel out the transcendent trace of inspired (less disciplined) moments. But it does imply that this trace can usually find articulation only through the diligence of determination. On the one hand, if we control the process too closely, our creations remain devoid of energy; on the other, if we surrender all structure, we lose the capacity to bring our inspiration to a viable expression. According to this view, creation is a delicate blend of self-surrender and an almost cruel degree of perseverance.

7

The art of living I have been promoting can be said to require a similar combination of self-surrender and discipline. This explains in part why this book has portrayed the matter from two seemingly opposed angles. If I started my analysis by focusing on the need to release the undisciplined energies of our being from underneath the constraints of our social persona, I have ended by looking at what it means to struggle with the volatile mixture of the two. In both instances, I have aligned character with the least socialized components of our being, yet as much as I want to pay tribute to the headiness of allowing these components to bubble up into the realm of sociality, I recognize that reaping the (long-term) benefits of this headiness usually requires the structure of social support systems. This is obvious to those who are interested in undertaking their art of living with the same deliberate perseverance as is demanded by other art forms. But it is equally applicable to those who merely wish to make it through the day. Generally speaking, one might say that self-loss—the surrender of rational consciousness that tends to mark moments when our social persona collapses—only makes sense if there is a self to lose in the first place. This is why it would be useless to talk about self-loss without also talking about the constellations of sociality that allow us to have a self to begin with and that, in addition, allow us to repeatedly revise this self. At the same time, our various attempts at self-fashioning can remain innovative (rather than purely mechanical) only to the extent that we are capable of entering into revitalizing states of self-loss.

The problem for many of us is that we are not very good at self-loss. Although we have been quite systematically socialized to maintain our disciplined persona, most of us have not had much training in the kind of self-surrender I have delineated in this chapter. Even those of us who are in principle capable of it often approach it with some trepidation. To the degree that it threatens our sense of ourselves as coherent individuals in control of our actions, and particularly to the degree that it raises the specter of untamed animality stripped of rational consciousness (the very specter that socialization aims to suppress), we may feel tempted to flee from it. This is how we sometimes come to reject the investments that most matter to us (that most faithfully capture the echo of the Thing). I have already acknowledged this rejection in relation to lovers (or potential lovers). But it is no less true of our other investments. We may feel uniquely enticed by certain kinds of investments, by certain kinds of objects and activities, yet hesitate to let ourselves be "conquered" by them, striving, instead, to neutralize their summons. Unfortunately, when we do this, when we recoil from objects and activities that call upon us in such a passionate manner, we destroy their capacity to turn our day into a space for the articulation of our idiom. Similarly, when we use the various objects and activities that the world makes available to us as mere means to an end, as inert tools or resources, their magic silently slips away; when we seek to stifle their disorienting alienness, we decline the invitation to aliveness that they extend to us.

The erotics of being I have highlighted here is so important in part because it helps us welcome this invitation. What is more, inasmuch as it animates the least socialized gradations of our being—the gradations that facilitate self-surrender—it almost automatically injects a dose of rebelliousness into our existence, so that even when we participate in social life, we do not allow ourselves to be engulfed by its most normative manifestations; it ensures that we do not become interchangeable with others no matter how fully "socialized," how fully a member of a given culture, we become. Undoubtedly, holding onto our character is becoming more difficult the more homogenized our society gets. But, fortunately for us, there are still people whose manner of living presupposes an ongoing rapport with the character-molding energies that course in the fissures of social life. Such individuals—individuals who have been able to integrate their character into their social makeup—tend to exude an existential tone that makes them appear uncompromisingly "themselves." This tone may be what we are referring to when we colloquially say that someone seems "comfortable in her skin." Such a person inhabits her character in ways that lend her being a singular (wholly inimitable) density. We find such individuals intriguing and are often drawn to them for seemingly inexplicable reasons. Their eccentricity entices us because we realize that if they are able to display it for all of us to see, it is because they are uncommonly courageous. After all, as we have learned, although being called to our character is genuinely exhilarating, it is also genuinely terrifying.

NOTES

PREFACE

1. *Reinventing the Soul: Posthumanist Theory and Psychic Life* (New York: Other Press, 2006); *A World of Fragile Things: Psychoanalysis and the Art of Living* (Albany: State University of New York Press, 2009); and *The Singularity of Being: Lacan and the Immortal Within* (New York: Fordham University Press, 2012).

1. THE CALL OF CHARACTER

1. I am obviously referring to Nietzsche's famous statement in *Thus Spoke Zarathustra*, trans. R. J. Hollingdale (London: Penguin, 1969).
2. In the realm of ethics, Kant was the one to formulate this notion most clearly by insisting that our ethical judgments must be "disinterested" in the sense of being devoid of all personal passions and investments.

See Immanuel Kant, *The Critique of Judgment*, trans. Werner S. Pluhar (New York: Hackett, 1987).

3. Bernard Williams, interviewed by Stuart Jeffries, *The Guardian*, November 30, 2002.

4. For an excellent analysis of this feeling, see Julia Kristeva, *New Maladies of the Soul*, trans. Ross Guberman (New York: Columbia University Press, 1995). See also my book *Reinventing the Soul: Posthumanist Theory and Psychic Life* (New York: Other Press, 2006).

5. On existential overagitation, see Jonathan Lear, *Happiness, Death, and the Remainder of Life* (Cambridge, Mass.: Harvard University Press, 2000). Eric L. Santner also makes a relevant argument in *On the Psychotheology of Everyday Life: Reflections on Freud and Rosenzweig* (Chicago: University of Chicago Press, 2001).

6. Adam Phillips explores our somewhat problematic attachment to the notion of a balanced life in *On Balance* (New York: Picador, 2011).

7. For a fascinating discussion of some of these issues, see Anthony Storr, *Solitude: A Return to the Self* (New York: Free Press, 2005).

2. THE PROCESS OF BECOMING

1. This perspective is common in popular spiritual writing. One of its most engaging articulations can be found in Thomas Moore's *Care of the Soul: A Guide for Cultivating Depth and Sacredness in Everyday Life* (New York: Harper Perennial, 1994).

2. The outlines of Nietzsche's thinking presented in this chapter are drawn primarily from *The Gay Science*, trans. Walter Kaufmann (New York: Vintage, 1974). The chapter epigraph is from page 335, emphasis in original. Note also the subtitle of Nietzsche's *Ecce Homo: How One Becomes What One Is*, trans. R. J. Hollingdale (New York: Penguin, 1992).

3. On falsely coherent selves, see D. W. Winnicott, "Ego Distortion in Terms of True and False Self," in *The Maturation Processes and the Facilitating Environment: Studies in the Theory of Emotional Development*, 140–152 (London: Karnac, 1965).

4. For a related examination of human life as an open-ended process, see Jonathan Lear, *Open-Minded: Working Out the Logic of the Soul* (Cambridge, Mass.: Harvard University Press, 1999).

5. This complicated argument exceeds the parameters of the present discussion. I plan to tackle it in a more academic book tentatively entitled *Between Levinas and Lacan: Self, Other, Ethics*.

6. One of my ongoing disagreements with contemporary theory is that it tends to paint the world as precisely such a default adversary. Those interested in how to conceptualize the world as a potentially enabling space of collective ideals might benefit from Lewis Kirshner's *Having a Life: Self-Pathology After Lacan* (Hillsdale, N.J.: The Analytic Press, 2004).

7. Slavoj Žižek talks about this feeling in a number of his books, but perhaps the most relevant in this context is *The Ticklish Subject: The Absent Centre of Political Ontology* (London: Verso, 2000).

3. THE SPECIFICITY OF DESIRE

1. I take my wording from Jean-Paul Sartre's *Being and Nothingness: An Essay in Phenomenological Ontology*, trans. Hazel Barnes (New York: Citadel, 2001).

2. Lauren Berlant, *Cruel Optimism* (Durham, N.C.: Duke University Press, 2011).

3. I am here drawing on Freud's famous essay "Mourning and Melancholia," in *The Standard Edition of the Complete Psychological Works of Sigmund Freud*, vol. 14, edited by James Strachey, 239–258 (New York: Norton, 1957).

4. The Lacanian insights in this chapter are drawn broadly from his work, but of specific interest are two of his seminars: *The Seminar of Jacques Lacan, Book VII: The Ethics of Psychoanalysis*, trans. Dennis Porter (New York: Norton, 1992), and *The Seminar of Jacques Lacan, Book XI: The Four Fundamental Concepts of Psychoanalysis*, trans. Alan Sheridan (New York: Norton, 1981).

5. Lacan, *The Ethics of Psychoanalysis*, 118.

6. The "disclosure"—or unveiling—of the world is a common theme in Heidegger's philosophy, attaining mystical dimensions in his later theory of poetic dwelling. See the essays collected in Martin Heidegger, *Poetry, Language, Thought*, trans. Albert Hofstadter (New York: Harper & Row, 1971).

7. See the final chapter of *The Four Fundamental Concepts of Psychoanalysis*.

8. Lacan, *The Ethics of Psychoanalysis*, 112.

9. Alenka Zupančič makes this point beautifully in *The Shortest Shadow: Nietzsche's Philosophy of the Two* (Cambridge, Mass.: MIT Press, 2003).

10. See Lacan, *The Ethics of Psychoanalysis*, chapter 24.

11. Ibid., 319.

12. I explore this problem in chapter 3 of *The Singularity of Being: Lacan and the Immortal Within* (New York: Fordham University Press, 2012).

13. I am here signaling to the idea that a desire that resuscitates the Thing's echo is a desire that relates to the Lacanian "real"—the part of our being that resists symbolization. See ibid.

4. THE BLUEPRINTS OF BEHAVIOR

1. My approach in this chapter is broadly Freudian. Those interested in the basics of his thinking might want to start with the following classics: *The Interpretation of Dreams*; *Five Lectures on Psychoanalysis*; *The New Introductory Lecture on Psychoanalysis*; *Beyond the Pleasure Principle*; *The Ego and the Id*; and *Civilization and Its Discontents*. These texts are available as separate volumes in *The Standard Edition of the Complete Psychological Works of Sigmund Freud* (New York: Norton).

2. Sigmund Freud, *Beyond the Pleasure Principle*, ed. James Strachey, in *The Standard Edition*, vol. 18 (New York: Norton, 1961), 23.

3. Freud characterized this state of unorganized desire as one of "polymorphous perversity" without thereby placing a normative judgment on it: it is simply the primordial, presocial manifestation of human wanting. See Sigmund Freud, *Three Essays on the Theory of Sexuality* (New York: Basic Books, 2000).

4. Jonathan Lear analyzes this predicament in *Therapeutic Action: An Earnest Plea for Irony* (New York: Other Press, 2004).

5. On the importance of developing an active relationship to our repetition compulsion, see Hand Loewald, *The Essential Loewald: Collected Papers and Monographs*, ed. Jonathan Lear (Hagerstown, Md.: University Publishing Group, 2000).

6. Lear argues along related lines throughout his work. See, in particular, his introduction to *The Essential Loewald*.

7. This point resides at the core of my argument in *A World of Fragile Things: Psychoanalysis and the Art of Living* (Albany: State University of New York Press, 2009).

5. THE ALCHEMY OF RELATIONALITY

1. Hannah Arendt, *The Origins of Totalitarianism* (New York: Harcourt Brace, 1966), 476.

2. Lacan makes this point in *The Seminar of Jacques Lacan, Book XI: The Four Fundamental Concepts of Psychoanalysis*, trans. Alan Sheridan (New York: Norton, 1981). But it is Laplanche who has developed it most extensively in *New Foundations of Psychoanalysis*, trans. David Macey (Oxford: Basil Blackwell, 1989). For more recent discussions of the enigmatic desire of the other, see Judith Butler, *Giving an Account of Oneself* (New York: Fordham University Press, 2005); Eric L. Santner, "Miracles Happen: Benjamin, Rosenzweig, Freud, and the Matter of the Neighbor," in *The Neighbor: Three Inquiries in Political Theology*, by Slavoj Žižek, Eric L. Santner, and Kenneth Reinhard, 76–133 (Chicago: University of Chicago Press, 2005); and Mari Ruti, *The Singularity of Being: Lacan and the Immortal Within* (New York: Fordham University Press, 2012).

3. I take up this issue in detail in my mainstream book *The Case for Falling in Love: Why We Can't Master the Madness of Love—and Why That's the Best Part* (Chicago: Sourcebooks Casablanca, 2011).

4. I discuss this summons in greater detail in *The Summons of Love* (New York: Columbia University Press, 2011).

5. On our culture's ambivalence about singleness, see Kate Bolick's delightful article "All the Single Ladies," *The Atlantic* (November 2011). See also Bella M. DePaulo, *Singled Out: How Singles Are Stereotyped, Stigmatized, and Ignored, and Still Live Happily Ever After* (New York: St. Martin's Griffin, 2007). For a more academic analysis, see Michael Cobb, *Single: Arguments for the Uncoupled* (New York: New York University Press, 2012).

6. See Arendt's *The Human Condition* (Chicago: University of Chicago Press, 1998) as well as *The Origins of Totalitarianism*.

7. Virginia Woolf, *A Room of One's Own* (New York: Harcourt Brace, 1991).

8. Stephen Mitchell argues along related lines in *Can Love Last? The Fate of Romance Over Time* (New York: Norton, 2003). I develop this line of reasoning about idealization in both *The Summons of Love* and *The Singularity of Being*.

9. My ideas about the sublime aspects of love have been influenced by Alenka Zupančič's *The Shortest Shadow: Nietzsche's Philosophy of the Two* (Cambridge, Mass.: MIT Press, 2003).

6. THE ETHICS OF RESPONSIBILITY

1. Kelly Oliver, *The Colonization of Psychic Space: A Psychoanalytic Social Theory of Oppression* (Minneapolis: University of Minnesota Press, 2004), 199.

2. Rhonda Byrne, *The Secret* (New York: Atria Books/Beyond Words, 2006).

3. For an incisive critique of "positive thinking" and of Byrne's book in particular, see Barbara Ehrenreich, *Bright-Sided: How Positive Thinking Is Undermining America* (New York: Picador, 2009). For a related critique, see Roy F. Baumeister and John Tierney, *Willpower: Rediscovering the Greatest Human Strength* (New York: Penguin, 2011).

4. This notion is perhaps most closely associated with Eckhart Tolle's influential *The Power of Now: A Guide to Spiritual Enlightenment* (Novato, Calif.: New World Library, 2004), but it has been enthusiastically embraced by the self-help industry, in particular its more spiritual echelons.

5. Nietzsche makes this argument in *On the Genealogy of Morals*, trans. Walter Kaufmann and R. J. Hollingdale (New York: Vintage, 1989), and *Unfashionable Observations*, trans. Richard T. Gray (Palo Alto, Calif.: Stanford University Press, 1995). For an excellent reading of Nietzsche's stance, see Alenka Zupančič, *The Shortest Shadow: Nietzsche's Philosophy of the Two* (Cambridge, Mass.: MIT Press, 2003).

6. For a sophisticated analysis of this impossibility, see Judith Butler, *Giving an Account of Oneself* (New York: Fordham University Press, 2005).

7. This theme can be found throughout Žižek's work, but one of its most pointed articulations is his critique of Levinasian ethics in "Neighbors and Other Monsters: A Plea for Ethical Violence," in *The Neighbor: Three Inquiries in Political Theology*, by Slavoj Žižek, Eric L. Santner, and Kenneth Reinhard, 134–190 (Chicago: University of Chicago Press, 2005).

8. For a related critique of Western notions of tolerance, see Wendy Brown, *Regulating Aversion: Tolerance in the Age of Identity and Empire* (Princeton, N.J.: Princeton University Press, 2006).

9. See Giorgio Agamben, *Remnants of Auschwitz: The Witness and the Archive*, trans. Daniel Heller-Roazen (Cambridge, Mass.: MIT Press, 1999).

10. Žižek, "Neighbors and Other Monsters," 185. See also Eric L. Santner's essay "Miracles Happen: Benjamin, Rosenzweig, Freud, and the Matter of the Neighbor," in *The Neighbor*, 76–133.

11. See Butler's *Giving an Account of Oneself* as well as *Precarious Life* (New York: Verso, 2004) and *Frames of War* (New York: Verso, 2009).

12. Butler makes this argument most forcefully in *Precarious Life* and *Frames of War*.

13. Butler, *Giving an Account of Oneself*, 42. See also my critique of Butler in the conclusion to *The Summons of Love* (New York: Columbia University Press, 2011).

14. Hannah Arendt, *The Human Condition* (Chicago: University of Chicago Press, 1998), 233, 237–241. For a related argument, see Julia Kristeva's *Intimate Revolt: The Powers and Limits of Psychoanalysis*, trans. Jeanine Herman (New York: Columbia University Press, 2002), and *Hatred and Forgiveness*, trans. Jeanine Herman (New York: Columbia University Press, 2010).

15. Oliver, *The Colonization of Psychic Space*, 195–200.

7. THE SWERVE OF PASSION

1. In what follows, I draw on the notion of the "truth-event" that Badiou develops throughout his work, but most accessibly in *Ethics: An Essay on the Understanding of Evil*, trans. Peter Hallward (London: Verso, 2001). Badiou is of course not the only contemporary philosopher to deploy the "event" as a way of thinking about radical change. The concept can be found in the work of Jacques Derrida and Gilles Deleuze, among others.

2. Badiou, *Ethics*, 52.

3. This, of course, is one of the central insights of Judith Butler's early work, in particular *Gender Trouble: Feminism and the Subversion of Identity* (New York: Routledge, 1990) and *Bodies That Matter: On the Discursive Limits of "Sex"* (New York: Routledge, 1993).

4. Alenka Zupančič makes a related argument in *The Shortest Shadow: Nietzsche's Philosophy of the Two* (Cambridge, Mass.: MIT Press, 2003).

8. THE UPSIDE OF ANXIETY

1. Theodor Adorno, *Minima Moralia: Reflections from Damaged Life*, trans. E. F. N. Jephcott (London: Verso, 2005), 62–63.

2. Ibid., 154.

3. See, for instance, Karl Marx, *The Economic and Philosophical Manuscripts of 1844*, trans. Martin Milligan (New York: Prometheus Books, 1988).

4. Adorno, *Minima Moralia*, 57–59.

5. Tim Dean, *Unlimited Intimacy: Reflections on the Subculture of Barebacking* (Chicago: University of Chicago Press, 2009), 60–62, 67–69.

6. This medicalization is obviously a part of what Michel Foucault, among others, has characterized as biopolitics: the social management of biological life. Readers unfamiliar with Foucault's thinking might want to look at *Essential Works of Foucault, 1954–1984*, 3 vols., ed. Robert Hurley et al. (New York: New Press, 1997).

7. Dean, *Unlimited Intimacy*, 190–191.

8. Expert readers should here recognize the echo of Heidegger's "being-toward-death" from *Being and Time*, trans. John Macquarrie and Edward Robinson (New York: Harper and Row, 1962). Yet they should also recall Emmanuel Levinas's vehement critique of this notion. For Levinas, it is not our own death that we should worry about, but rather the death of the other. On this, see Levinas, *Entre Nous: On Thinking-of-the-Other*, trans. Michael B. Smith and Barbara Harshav (New York: Columbia University Press, 1998).

9. Adam Phillips addresses this issue eloquently in *Darwin's Worms: On Life Stories and Death Stories* (New York: Basic Books, 2000).

10. Adorno, *Minima Moralia*, 59.

11. Hannah Arendt, *The Human Condition* (Chicago: University of Chicago Press, 1998), 180–181.

9. THE EROTICS OF BEING

1. Christopher Bollas, *Being a Character: Psychoanalysis and Self-Experience* (New York: Routledge, 1993), 30.

2. Ibid., 31.

3. I make this argument in a more academic vein in *The Singularity of Being: Lacan and the Immortal Within* (New York: Fordham University Press, 2012). My analysis has been influenced by Alenka Zupančič's *Ethics of the Real: Kant, Lacan* (London: Verso, 2000).

4. Roland Barthes, *Camera Lucida: Reflections on Photography* (New York: Hill & Wang, 1992).

5. Bollas, *Being a Character*, 17.

INDEX